Two studies on ethnic group relations in Africa:
Senegal, the United Republic of Tanzania

Two studies
on ethnic group relations
in Africa

Senegal
The United Republic of
Tanzania

Unesco Paris 1974

Published by the
United Nations Educational,
Scientific and Cultural Organization,
7 Place de Fontenoy, 75700 Paris
Printed by P. Attinger SA, Neuchâtel

ISBN 92-3-101101-4
French edition: 92-3-201101-8

Preface

Studies of trends in ethnic group relations in various parts of the world are among the major components of the Unesco programme on race over the next few years. This book contains the first two such studies.

The term 'ethnic group' is here broadly defined, and used for any segment of a society which is considered as differing from others in it because of differences in culture, language or physical characteristics; the studies accordingly cover both 'race relations' and 'tribal relations'.

Senegal and the United Republic of Tanzania were selected to illustrate some of the immediately post-colonial problems in African States as—during a period of rapid social change—they build nations out of diverse groups.

The period covered is roughly 1969 to 1970; nothing after 1970 is included. Both studies were made in the countries concerned: in Senegal, by Fatoumata-Agnès Diarra and Pierre Fougeyrollas of the University of Dakar and, in the United Republic of Tanzania, by Yash Ghai, Paul Puritt, Gerhart K. Grohs and Simon Mbilinyi of the University of Dar es Salaam.

No attempt was made to standardize approach or presentation. Nevertheless, certain common patterns emerge.

The post-colonial society in both, following independence, involves relationships between European settlers, European immigrants of recent date, and expatriate advisers, and the African society in which they now live.

None of these groups is wholly self-contained. Status is nowhere coincident with race (except in so far as there are no working-class whites). Conflict between groups still exists but it differs widely in degree and scope.

Colonialism also left a particular type of class stratification. Ethnic groups fitted into a well-defined hierarchy: the stratification has been modified by political independence, changes in the status of groups and classes within the groups.

Ethnically different trading groups whose members are linked by kinship form a special case, particularly if they are recent immigrants.

More needs to be known about tribal formation, tribal economics and the formation of social institutions; these matters will be dealt with in greater detail in subsequent studies.

The opinions expressed in this book are solely those of the authors and do not necessarily reflect the views of the Secretariat.

Contents

Part One
Ethnic group relations in Senegal

by Fatoumata-Agnès Diarra and Pierre Fougeyrollas

Part One
Ethnic group relations in Senegal

by Fatoumata-Agnès Diarra and Pierre Fougeyrollas

Introduction

Words and facts

The two processes of modernization and decolonization are, at the present time, the decisive factors in the emergence and crystallization of national societies in Africa. This means that the traditional societies of the past are being subjected to twofold pressures in the direction both of aggregation and of segregation.

These traditional societies comprised peoples or parts of peoples to which the term ethnic could legitimately be applied. Today, certain ethnic groups are being irresistibly impelled towards uniting with one another to form a new group which is national in the true sense of the word. At the same time, however, the same ethnic group may find itself torn apart, with one section being drawn in to form part of one national entity while another is attracted into another sphere of national influence.

The artificiality of the frontiers between African States, resulting from colonial divisions, can neither conceal nor adequately explain the regroupings and partitions referred to.

In addition, contemporary African societies include foreign or marginal population components left over from the colonial period. Their integration or rejection is, quite clearly, a burning issue.

In Africa, as elsewhere, the traditional societies comprised men who shared a whole set of technological, linguistic and cultural features which were the distinguishing marks of a people or ethnic group. Although the word is still used by various non-African observers, the tribe ceased quite a long time ago to play an important part in the traditional or transitional societies of Africa. It should be made clear that the tribe never represents the whole life of the traditional society; it is merely a subdivision or institutionalized section within a people or ethnic group.

In point of fact, in most present-day African societies, the tribe scarcely survives except in the form of patronymics which are a reminder of the tribes of long ago. It is quite ridiculous to speak of tribal warfare in Nigeria when the antagonists, as in the case of the Yoruba and the Ibo, number more than 10 million men or when, as in the case of the Hausa, we have a people or ethnic group comprising several tens of millions.

In Senegal, for example, it is easy to distinguish the peoples or ethnic groups which have gone to make up the present Senegalese nation, but the tribes which used to exist within each of these ethnic groups have now practically disappeared.[1]

In fact, far from being scientific descriptions of an actual state of affairs, 'tribe', 'tribal' and 'tribalism' are ideological terms tending, consciously or unconsciously, to discredit the peoples and nations of Africa in the eyes of foreigners or even, through the operation of an all too familiar process of alienation, in the eyes of certain Africans.

By inter-ethnic relations, we thus mean those existing between the peoples or ethnic groups of which the Senegalese national society is formed, just as we would speak of the relations between Bavarians, Rhinelanders, Saxons and natives of Baden-Württemberg in the Federal Republic of Germany.

By interracial relations, we mean those existing between the members of the various black African ethnic groups in Senegal, on the one hand, and the wholly or partly foreign elements established in the country, on the other.

We do not, of course, attribute any scientific value to the concept of race where human beings are involved. We simply note that, in relation to Senegalese society, certain elements are still marked by various features indicative of their foreign origin and non-integration. It is diversity of culture far more than difference in pigmentation which is involved here. Nevertheless, it is true that,

1. In June 1968, a French journalist rather oddly defined the Serer as the tribe to which the President of the Republic belonged, whereas they are a people or ethnic group numbering 700,000 and forming part of the emerging Senegalese nation.

when the two are combined, a difference in pigmentation then assumes a historical importance which allows the observer, in the interests of brevity, to speak of interracial relations between the various communities in the modern society which is taking shape.

In the interviews which follow, no reference is made—and for very good reason—to tribes or tribal differences. On the other hand, references to race will be found. In these cases, one of two things may be meant: the difference in pigmentation between black and white may be in question, which is easy to understand, even though the term race is unsatisfactory and full of dangerous ambiguities; or else the word race may be used to designate an ethnic group. It was, in fact, the colonial system which, by treating colonial peoples as zoological specimens, gave spurious currency to this misuse.

The misleading uses of the terms 'tribe' and 'race' must be eradicated from modern parlance, and the words 'people' or 'ethnic group' and 'national society' introduced instead, with all the regard for exactitude recommended above. This would be extremely beneficial both to science and to mankind, for the inter-ethnic and interracial tensions being experienced by African societies today are, in the end, less serious than the alienating ideas about them kept alive by hurried journalists or by pseudo-scholars.

The method used

The method used for this survey was the semi-directed interview. This means that the interviewers were not tied to rigid sets of cut-and-dried questions, but equally were not thrown on their own resources for dealing with respondents: actually they organized their interviews from a survey guide indicating in their order the themes on which subjects should be interrogated.

In the event, our interviewers saw fifty-eight people of Senegalese origin (ten Wolof, ten Serer, eight Tukulor, two Fulani, twelve Mandingo, ten Diola, six Lébou), eight Moors, nine Euro-African or Afro-Asian mixed bloods, twenty-four Lebanese and ten French, making a total of 109 individuals.

By drawing names by lot, a degree of variety was achieved as regards sex, age, religion and social and occupational status of subjects. However, there was not enough time to take a proper sample of Senegal's population and our results are accordingly indicative rather than representative.[1]

We sought to determine the images formed of each other by the ethnic groups and also by the Senegalese and aliens among them. We discovered a number of stereotypes, i.e. fixed and quasi-identical 'images' harboured by all interviewees of a given ethnic or race group, and it is precisely this stereotypic character of the images thus brought to light that inclines us to think that we have discovered consistent, persistent and important psycho-social data. It should be added that the results of our 1969 survey have been confirmed by the other investigations of the Department of Social Psychology of IFAN (Institut Fondamental d'Afrique Noire).

Before discussing these results, a few facts about Senegalese society should be given. The population of Senegal is now more than 3.5 million. Of these, 1.5 million are Wolof, 700,000 Serer, 500,000 Tukulor, 300,000 Fulani, 250,000 Mandingo, 200,000 Diola and 40,000 Lébou, not to speak of other minorities related to the major ethnic groups just named. Besides these African Negro groups, constituting the bulk of the national society, there are marginal groups such as the Moors (under 50,000), Cape Verde islanders and Portuguese or blacks from territories under Portuguese rule (under 10,000), Lebanese (roughly 10,000) and French (currently under 30,000).

Ninety per cent of Senegalese are Muslim and 80 per cent country dwellers. The official language of the republic is French, while Wolof, which really is a people's national language, is spoken or understood by more than 75 per cent of the population.

The old capital, St Louis (Ndar), and the new, Dakar, are in regions with large Wolof majorities; from St Louis to Dakar, and from Diourbel to Kaolack, is practically continuous, fairly densely peopled Wolof country. It is therefore not surprising that in Senegal the national society should have based itself first and foremost on the Wolof people and their language (without, on that account, implying that they are an oppressive ethnic group). Further, the Serer, who live in and around the regions of Sine-Saloum and Thiès, are increasingly taking on a Wolof linguistic and cultural imprint.

1. A selection of these interviews is published in this volume.

Thus Wolof and the increasingly 'Wolofized' Serer are at once the two largest ethnic groups in Senegal and a kind of nucleus of the national society that is taking shape.

On the borders of the country are three ethnic groups which straddle the frontier lines: in the north, the Tukulor, in the east and south-east, the Mandingo, and in the south-west, the Diola. The Tukulor were the propagators of Islam and on this account they enjoy special esteem in Senegal, where they are still thought of as the ethnic group of the great marabout families. Another interesting point is that, according to tradition, the Tukulor and the Serer are related and likewise the Serer and the Diola.

Thus in the background of the modernizing Wolof–Serer conjunct, we glimpse a chain of great antiquity linking the Serer to the Tukulor of the Sahel and the Diola of the forests; unquestionably, part at least of Senegal's national unity derives from this. As regards the Mandingo (Malinké, Bambara, Socé, Sarakolé), they are the bridge between Senegal and the Sudanese hinterland, that is, the depths of continental Africa. Lastly we must recall the Fulani, found scattered throughout Senegal, who share a common language with the Tukulor, and through whom Senegal can communicate with a diversity of West African and even North Cameroonian peoples. As we see, between population elements which were different but related, cultural and linguistic ties developed which were to issue, after the testing colonial period, in the national society of today.

In relation to the ethnic groups we have been discussing, the Moors (of Senegalese or Mauritanian nationality), who speak an Arabic dialect (Hassania), the Portuguese-speakers from Cape Verde, and from Portugal itself, the Arabic-speaking Lebanese, and the French, are marginal or foreign elements. It is for this reason we have used the term 'inter-ethnic' for relations between Senegal's black African groups, and 'interracial' for the relations between the black elements and the others. Most of the Moors and a lot of the Cape Verde islanders, Portuguese and Lebanese speak or understand Wolof and, generally, the language of communication of a particular region, while the French, with very few exceptions, remain impervious to African languages. It should finally be noted that the Moors and Lebanese are mostly small or middling traders (though some of the Lebanese are large-scale merchants) while the French fill economically privileged positions inherited from the old colonial set-up (industry, commerce, executive and management posts in the public and private sectors).

The present economic situation and the clash of Senegalese nationalism and the foreign interests still present in the country make it possible to understand our most general conclusion that in Senegal we have to think in terms of inter-ethnic peace and inter-racial tensions.

A terminological question remains to be dealt with: the word 'tribe'. Often journalists and even ethnologists confuse the notions of 'ethnic group' and 'tribe', and use 'tribe' when they mean 'ethnic group'. An ethnic group or people is the total factuality of a traditional society. It presents community of language though without excluding a degree of dialectal diversity; it presents a common pattern of technical and economic activities; lastly, it presents community of culture, formerly expressed in the traditional religion of each particular society. Thus the Wolof, the Serer, the Tukulor, and the Diola are ethnic groups or, more accurately, they were separate peoples before beginning to amalgamate in the emerging national society of Senegal. The tribe, on the other hand, is a fissiparous institution of the traditional society. Just as in ancient times the Hebrew people were divided into twelve tribes, so the peoples or ethnic groups of Africa have experienced division into tribes. In Senegal today, the traces of a former division into tribes are still discoverable among the Diola and Tukulor; it would be harder to find them among the Wolof or the Serer.

War between the tribes forming a single ethnic group was part of the activities of the old traditional societies, but has long since passed out of fashion. The conflicts between Africans today have nothing tribal about them; they are inter-ethnic, or even inter-national. In Senegal, the term 'tribe' is not used but its use in the Cameroons, to designate the Bamileke, the Fulani, the Ewrondo and the Boulou is, beyond question, wholly incorrect; for these are peoples who once had their own internal divisions into tribes, and to-day are ethnic, not tribal, components of the Cameroonian 'nation'.

The misuse of the term 'tribe' is as harmful for Africa, particularly abroad, as was the use of 'race' elsewhere, applied to designate collections of human beings claimed to be homogeneous.

In trying to assess the degree of understanding or lack of it between the groups forming the present-day society of Senegal, we judged it sufficient to rely on the notion of inter-ethnic relations. The notion of inter-race relations was resorted to with reference to the marginal and foreign elements, but with no presumption either way regarding the alleged existence of homogeneous races.

The ethnic groups of Senegal and their interrelations

In the social life of Senegal, as of any other country, it is possible to distinguish a conventionalized and—as it were—official level, and an everyday level. At the official level, ethnic groups as such are not taken into consideration; ministers, civil servants and clerks are appointed without regard to their ethnic origins. At the everyday level, however, these origins are of great importance. In ordinary conversation, the person we meet is often apostrophized as 'Tukulor', 'Diola', 'Serer', 'Fulani' or 'Wolof', and ethnic origin is frequently cited in describing personality. Similarly, a large proportion of the quips so numerous in conversation between Senegalese turn on the qualities and defects attributed to each person by reason of his ethnic origin.

There are no disputes or tensions between the ethnic groups of Senegal, but every Senegalese has a set of stereotypes providing—as it were—'Identikit' pictures of his own ethnic group and the others. When our interviewers asked subjects what they thought of their own and the other ethnic groups, they obtained replies which were closely similar because they reflected not varying individual experience, but stereotypes of very ancient origin. We therefore propose to run through the principal ethnic groups of Senegal exhibiting each one's image of itself and of the others.

The Wolof, like the other ethnic groups, generally have a high opinion of themselves. They consider that they are intelligent and have a great talent for social adjustment, and above all that modern Senegal is mainly of their making. They further claim to be good Moslems.

In actual fact, the Wolof are the Senegalese people who, in the past, have had the most contacts with foreigners and have become the most intensely involved in the urban life of centres such as St Louis and Dakar. Their feeling that they are particularly intelligent and particularly adaptable would seem to stem from this historic situation.

The fact that the Wolof language has become the national mass language of two-thirds of the country also contributes to giving the Wolof a special 'pride of group'. They do not oppress the other ethnic groups, but they have a tendency to believe themselves more fundamentally Senegalese than the others. At bottom they often identify their ethnicity and their nationality. But if we go on from the most spontaneous expression of feelings to forms of more pondered response, Wolof interviewees reply that a Tukulor, Serer, Diola or Mandingo can be just as good a Senegalese as a Wolof.

The rejoinder to the Wolof's ethno-national pride is furnished by the reactions of the other ethnic groups. The Tukulor, Serer, Diola and Mandingo not infrequently tax the Wolof with arrogance, with excessive love of money, or even with bad faith. These are the reactions of more substantially rural ethnic groups towards the more frequently urbanized Wolof and, in a word, the Serer, Tukulor or Mandingo peasant is suspicious of the Wolof civil servant, clerk or small tradesman for whom, as for Europeans, money has become an overriding consideration.

The Tukulor frequently stigmatize the Wolof as less pious, and worse Moslems than themselves, while the Serer and Diola consider them less hard-working. More generally, the members of the non-Wolof ethnic groups are almost always at one in criticizing the Wolof, which does not, however, stop them from speaking Wolof or consenting, at least to a certain extent, to cultural 'Wolofization'.

It is clear that the Wolof have a special place in the Senegal of today. They identify themselves with the country, with the rest following their lead in a diversity of new behaviour patterns. However, the rest make them pay in some sort for their primacy by subjecting them to continuous criticism and raillery.

The stereotypes we have been discussing do not preclude marriages between Wolof and Tukulor, Mandingo or Serer, provided that both partners are Muslims.

The Serer often give evidence of feeling that they constitute or used to constitute what might be called the quintessential Senegal. In effect, having remained peasants or fishermen, they have maintained far fewer foreign contacts and are considerably less urbanized than the Wolof.

The qualities claimed by the Serer are not so much intelligence and adaptability as loyalty to tradition and love of work. Mostly

Moslems, with a Catholic minority, they have preserved the traditional black African heritage of the customs and representations which play a part in their notion of themselves. For the Serer, the Wolof are cultural hybrids, while they in their rural life have remained more genuinely African and Senegalese.

Naturally, as we have said, the Serer are being subjected to Wolof cultural and linguistic influences; they are suffering this transformation somewhat reluctantly but without hostility. For them, the Wolof is a kind of intermediary between the tradition which is theirs and an alien pattern of modernization which is increasingly regarded as bound to come. The ethnic pride of the Serer derives more from a sense of history than from a sense of destiny. Hence it does not exclude receptivity to the transformations of which the Wolof were at once the first beneficiaries and the first agents.

Among the Tukulor and Diola, opinions of the Serer are most often very favourable. Both peoples invoke the legendary kinship with the Serer which confers that reciprocal right of friendly abuse that is known to anthropologists as the *parenté à plaisanteries* (teasing kinship).

To the Tukulor the Serer are above all hard-working and faithful, signifying that they respected the Serer even when they themselves were already Muslim, while the Serer still followed their traditional black African religion. To the Diola, the Serer are religious and loyal beings. In other words, the Diola regard the Serer as very close to them, in virtue even of the traditional religion of which the two peoples practised related variants.

In Wolof eyes, the Serer are somewhat hidebound by non-Islamic beliefs and traditionalism, scorned by the citizens of Dakar and St Louis. The Wolof are none the less sensible of the progress being made by their language and the Muslim religion in Serer country. In the final count, the ethnic difference between Wolof and Serer tends to decrease or even disappear, giving place to a 'Senegalization' which is turning out to be largely 'Wolofization'. More and more, the Serer's stereotypes of the Wolof and the Wolof's of the Serer centre around a certain relative discord between the more tradition-bound countryman and the townsman more intensely harried by modernization.

The Tukulor cultural personality remains a strong one. They regard themselves as the missionaries *par excellence* of Islam in

Senegal. In their consciousness, their 'Africanness' and 'Islamicness' are co-mingled.

The virtues they revere are those of the saint and the warrior: faith in Islam, moral and physical courage, and the sense of honour which in everyday life expresses the first two. The hero epitomizing the Tukulor virtues is El Hadj Omar Tall, the founder of a vast empire during the nineteenth century.

A marginal group in relation to Senegal, the Tukulor are historically an integral part of Sudano-Sahelian Africa, and have an even stronger ethnic pride than the Wolof. The remaining point is that, whereas the Wolof's pride is in mobility and adaptation, that of the Tukulor is in African tradition in its Islamic variant. Given piety and loyalty, the rest seems to them by comparison secondary or even insignificant. With the Fulani, to whom they are closely related, the Tukulor are nostalgic for an African empire which may have stretched from the banks of the River Senegal to Northern Cameroon. Less frequently 'Wolofized' than the Serer, the Tukulor are nevertheless active partners in a Senegal of which they feel they can still be the educators.

The Wolof response to this Tukulor self-portrait is an attitude at once admiring and critical. Although the Wolof consider themselves good Muslims, they unhesitatingly rate the Tukulor as exemplary Muslims; they know how much the spread of Islam in Senegal owes to the Tukulor marabouts. That much conceded, the Wolof are conscious that the religious and warlike values of the Tukulor are no longer those predominating in a contemporary world in process of modernization. In St Louis and Dakar the Tukulor was yesterday the water-carrier and today is often the street trader. Thus the Wolof regard the Tukulor as archaic, backward, even sometimes hypocritical in their obstinate defence of a tradition forced on to the ropes by social evolution.

The Serer take a much more favourable view of the Tukulor as a result of the reputed kinship already mentioned. The Diola, by reason of their links with the Serer, share the latter's opinion of the Tukulor, while the Mandingo are often found to be impressed by the Tukulor's historically exemplary Islamism.

The Fulani, who became Islamic missionaries after having fought against the faith for a good while, regard themselves, like the Tukulor, as men of faith and courage. The other groups accept this, while at the same time criticizing what is deemed their arrogance and archaism. Generally speaking, the Fulani, in Senegal, are regarded with less admiration and are more readily criticized than the Tukulor. The reason is that, in the final count, the Tukulor are essentially of Senegal, whereas the Fulani are common to the whole West African complex.

The Diola, again, while long regarded by the Wolof as backward, 'pagan' and followers of rather dangerous beliefs, have, over the last ten years, been powerfully drawn into the national society.

Like the Serer, they see themselves above all as hard-working, honest peasants. They believe in the virtue of work. In Dakar, they take the subordinate jobs and are known for their conscientiousness and regular habits. The qualities they claim for themselves are usually conceded by the other groups. The Serer regard them as kinsmen, the Tukulor treat them as kinsmen of kinsmen, and the Wolof pay tribute to their hard-working qualities. Better still, the Diolas' Mohammedanism, formerly disputed, is today acknowledged by the other Muslims of Senegal. It is true that a fairly large Diola minority adopted Roman Catholicism while the older elements of the ethnic group are still faithful to the traditional religion of black Africa, but this has not prevented a favourable opinion of this people from developing.

There remain the Mandingo, who are very faithful to the beliefs and practices of Islam. They too, hold by the religious and warlike values, although this conviction is in general less visceral, because of more recent date, than in the case of the Tukulor or the Fulani.

These Mandingo elements (Bambara, Malinké, Soninké of Eastern Senegal and Socé of Upper Casamance) temper their religious and warlike fervour with solid peasant virtues. Among them piety and courage are ballasted by the taste for rural employments (agricultural or pastoral).

For all these reasons, they are highly thought of by the Tukulor, Serer and Diola. The Wolof tend to regard the Mandingo as backward, but the severity of this judgement, or rather presumption, is tempered by acknowledgement of the Muslim piety of those judged. In a sense, the Mandingo are 'Sudanese', somewhat out of place in Senegal. But for this very reason they enjoy a status which is that of both brothers and good neighbours. There seems little likelihood of tracing any tension between them and their neighbours or even a critical attitude of any severity towards them.

To conclude, the Senegalese ethnic group's image of itself and of the other groups reveal two systems of values: on the one hand, the traditional system whose values, in Senegal, as in the whole Sudano-Sahelian area, are black African Islamic (piety, courage, sense of honour) and, on the other hand, a more recent system with values appropriate to progressive modernization (application at work, honest dealing, professional efficiency). The Tukulor and the Fulani are the greatest exponents of the traditional values and the Diola and the Serer of the values of progressive modernization.

It is fairly obvious that the Wolof want the best of both worlds: they want to be first in piety, courage and honour after the manner of the Tukulor who converted them to Islam, and in occupational efficiency after the manner of the Diola and the Serer from whom they have learnt to lay claim to virtues in this respect. The Wolof want to epitomize all the qualities, just as they want Wolof and Senegal to be synonyms. By way of reaction, the others, i.e. the Tukulor, Serer and Diola, could tend to deny them any identity or, at the best, to rate them as an ethnic hotchpotch without any character of its own.

Luckily for the Wolof and for the Senegalese national society, the Tukulor, Serer and Diola, with the Mandingo, have had a long training in understanding each other. This background works towards a many-sided receptivity which also embraces the Wolof despite some adverse stereotypes.

There was no survey of the Lébou, the original population of the Dakar area now absorbed into the Wolof mass, nor of the Bassari, on the borders of Guinea, following a set-pattern traditional way of life. Despite this omission, our survey led us to feel that the cohesive pull of the national society is already greater than the pull of the ethnic groups. The stereotypes subsist, but are easily overridden by the sense of national unity.

The Moors in Senegal

In the Wolof language, the word 'Nar' is used to designate the Arabs and even the Semites as a whole; the Moors are labelled 'Nar Ganar'. Their Muslim faith and familiar use of the Wolof language enable them to adjust without difficulty to the Senegalese *milieu*. But their functions in retail trade put them in a special position with regard to the consumer in Senegal.

In Moorish shops there are a host of food and household items sold in small quantities to fit the day-to-day requirements and low spending power of the housewife. The shopkeeper also sells on credit. He is therefore often needed but often taxed with profiteering. It is on this basis that the place of the Moors of Senegal in the life of the society is that of marginal elements rather than of foreigners.

The Moors regard themselves more as members of the extensive Arab community than of the African community proper. Their special pride is the use of the Arabic dialect which is their mother tongue. On occasion we encountered Moors who evinced a sense of superiority over Senegal's black African ethnic groups, while it must not be forgotten that in Mauritania conflicts have sometimes set the Moors and the Tukulor living on the right bank of the River Senegal at each other's throats.

However, it is only fair to say that the Moors living in Senegal are extremely well adjusted to the ambient society. Most of them prefer the Wolof to the other Senegalese, perhaps because of both group's bent for trading.

The Wolof regard the Moors with some mistrust. In the past the Moors had the reputation of stealing black children to make slaves of them. However, times have changed greatly, for none of our informants produced this old stereotype. The mistrust today is that of the consumer towards the retailer with whom he is in direct daily contact.

This apart, the Senegalese frequently criticize the Moors for carelessness in dress and even dirtiness. In fact we noted a sharp contrast between the taste of the Senegalese in general, of either sex, and of the Wolof in particular, for the elegant ceremonial costumes of black Africa and for personal grooming and the Moor's Saharan simplicity of dress. The Moors are as economical over clothes as over everything else and often wear their garments 'till they fall apart', hence the reactions of the Wolof and others.

To the Moor's feeling of ethnic superiority over the blacks of Senegal, the latter respond by a tacit sense of superiority on other grounds. We need only consider the Saharan environment of the Moors and the urban setting of the Wolof of Dakar and St Louis to appreciate frictions which, in Senegal, do not reach the level of conflict or even of serious tension. There are marriages between Moors and Wolof; Moors sometimes take Wolof wives, and Wolofs sometimes marry Moorish women. Here Islam makes it possible to rise above a difference that is not only ethnic. The future of the Moors in Senegal will probably depend on their ability to become employable in sectors other than trade.

The Lebanese in Senegal

Of those known as Lebanese in Senegal a majority really are Lebanese and a minority Syrian; among the true Lebanese both Muslims and Christians are found. This Lebanese-Syrian group occupy mercantile positions ranging from small shopkeeping to large-scale commerce. Most of them are in an average way of business only, but a few families are among the leaders of the business community. Thus the Lebanese are in competition both with the Senegalese at the middle level of commerce and with the French in big business. Finally a proportion of them practise liberal professions such as law, medicine, etc.

It was during the colonial period that the Lebanese arrived in various West African countries, including Senegal, to seek their fortune as traders. Thus the colonial situation was an inducement to them to approximate their manner of life and way of thinking to that of the French, i.e. the dominant foreign stratum of the society of the day.

Traces of this situation subsist today in the attitudes of the Lebanese interviewed. Most of them regard themselves as foreigners, and in any case as closer to the French than to the Africans. On the other hand, some of them admit that they have far more to do with the Senegalese than with the French in the way of business and that they have ended up by looking on Senegal, up to a point, as home.

The Lebanese are conscious that they are Arabs; and some of the youngest are militants in the Arab cause. But most of the traders questioned are primarily conscious, on their own showing, of the division of the society into blacks and whites. And it is to the white minority that they are anxious to belong, to the point of propositions which are sometimes racialist.

Our Lebanese informants often hold to it that the Senegalese are incapable of running a commercial or industrial undertaking and denigrate their efforts to develop. Some go as far as condemning intermarriage between Lebanese and Africans. Basically they have not got over the colonial traumatism.

Clearly there are exceptions; some Lebanese interviewed said that Senegal had become far more their real country than the Lebanon from which they came. And this attitude may bring about the integration into the national Senegalese community of those Lebanese who have chosen to remain in the country.

For the present, race prejudice and even racialism are clouding the vision of all too many Lebanese with regard to the Senegalese among whom they live. The persistence of these prejudices inherited from colonial days is undoubtedly due to fear of losing what are often favoured economic positions. Asserting or believing that the Africans are still not fit to manage businesses is a cheap way of justifying the maintenance of the privileged situations enjoyed by some Lebanese traders. It is therefore a reasonable assumption that the accession of Senegalese to managerial posts will create the essential condition for the elimination of the prejudices just described.

From the Senegalese side, those questioned most frequently regarded the Lebanese as foreigners, enterprising indeed, but grasping and all too often infected with race prejudice. On occasion one gets criticisms of the Lebanese on moral and religious grounds: it is known that a proportion of them are Muslim and it is considered that they are too slack over the Koranic rules, with drinking, neglect of alms-giving, and the daily prayers skimped or omitted.

For a proportion of Senegalese the Lebanese are whites but without the qualities conceded, for example, to the French. It is indeed this view that the Lebanese seek to counter by trying to identify with the French, who constitute the white community *par excellence* in Senegal. Closer to the Senegalese than most of the French, the Lebanese are, for that very reason, criticized more sharply. It is not an exaggeration to speak of tensions, albeit latent rather than manifest, between the Lebanese and the Senegalese. The worsening of the economic situation and the sharpening of commercial competition might one day, despite the habitual tolerance of the Senegalese, bring these two groups into conflict.

The French in Senegal

In the days of the colonial régime, the French and the Senegalese coexisted, the former as rulers, and the latter as ruled, without, in most cases, developing personal relations of any substance. The significance of this is that while there was no lack of business relations between the two sides, culturally each group ordered its life according to criteria completely alien to the other. Even the minority of Senegalese most strongly subjected to French influence developed a range of inter-personal relationships with Europeans in which close and sustained relations were an exception. The latter took the form of mixed marriages principally in St Louis, the resulting metis group will be discussed on a later page.

Most of the French now living in Senegal are inheritors, consciously or unconsciously, of the old colonial situation. Those whom our interviewers met very frequently expressed themselves as 'disappointed' in the Senegalese. They came—they said— to the country to help in its development and they did not feel that they had found among the Africans the energy, the pride in their work, or even the patriotism, to produce this development. Consequently, many of the French think poorly of the Senegalese and some evince racialist attitudes, even though less crudely expressed than among some of the Lebanese.

Actually, lack of understanding of the facts of African culture is the dominant influence in the opinions of the French in Senegal. To this minority, family life, polygamy, the sense of the traditional ceremonies, even the Muslim religion itself, are so many total or near-total mysteries. It is as though the French in Senegal were faulting the Senegalese for not resembling the French in every detail.

The dominant positions still occupied by the French in industry, commerce, the universities and some liberal professions contribute powerfully to making them think themselves irreplaceable and to fostering the dangerous illusion that the Senegalese could not take over their responsibilities in their stead. Naturally this tendency is aggravated among whites in subordinate posts who are more threatened than the others by the process of 'Senegalization'.

In general, the French interviewed grant the Senegalese the qualities of hospitality, friendliness and kindness, and they are impressed by the elegance of the Senegalese women. But they do not believe that the Senegalese have the virtues required for success in the enterprise of development and modernization. Lastly it was noted that some of the French generalized in their judgements of the 'Senegalese', while others made a distinction between the Wolof on the one hand and the country's other ethnic groups, notably the Serer and the Diola, considering the Wolof arrogant, lazy and of low ability and the others hard-working and likeable. Here we are back at the colonial stereotypes of the 'good nigger' and the 'bad nigger'. In fact the Wolof, more often town-dwellers and politically awake, have struck the Europeans as less manageable than the Serer or Diola peasants, and this is undoubtedly at the back of the images we have instanced.

On the Senegalese side, views of Europeans generally, and the French in particular, are not without ambivalences. The European, particularly in urban circles, is fairly often looked on as pretentious, aggressive and even racialist, but nevertheless a certain number of his behaviour patterns continue to be copied.

The Senegalese peasants, discontented with the functioning of the co-operatives and State agricultural agencies, sometimes say, not without humour, that they need the French managers back; they do not in any case seem to evince any hostility towards nationals of the former colonial power and look to them for various forms of assistance. On the other hand, there are large numbers of Senegalese civil servants, merchants, executives and heads of businesses who are increasingly irked by the presence of Frenchmen at the head of things and in appointments as technical advisers or even technical assistants. Here the tensions are manifest, with a latent threat of conflict between Senegalese and French. There is a risk of national feelings arising that may, if thwarted by the obstinacy of privileged foreign elements, lead in the fairly near future to explosions.

It is possible for the Senegalese upper strata to continue to maintain good relations with the French living in France if the French in Senegal do not bar the way to their social advancement and their achievement of responsibility for running things. This problem is no longer one of social relations, but of government policy.

The Senegalese have long known or felt that the French living in their country were, with very few exceptions, incapable of understanding their culture and recognizing it as such. This does not prevent their being tolerant and adopting some features of European culture in its French form, but their tolerance will not continue for long as regards the management and the executive staffing in establishments in their country. In these areas, competition between Senegalese and nationals of the former colonial power may very quickly jeopardize their mutual relations. The image that the Senegalese have of the French is still ambivalent; there is a danger of it hardening under the pressure of instances of unfair competition and rivalry. For a real dialogue with the former colonizers or their present progeny, the Senegalese need first to become genuinely masters of the means of their national development.

The metis

In Senegal, as elsewhere, the metis are in a special situation, attracted and, more or less, rejected by the two communities from which they descend. During the colonial period, it was frequent for metis to be tempted to join in the life and culture of the European population. Since the country has acceded to sovereign nationhood, some of them have tried to integrate into Senegalese society.

Those we caused to be interviewed in many instances expressed, very forcibly, their sense of particularity, declaring that it was difficult to be a metis because of one's rejection to varying degrees by both whites and blacks. This doubly marginal situation quite often leads them to pass favourable judgements on the whites and unfavourable on the blacks.

The urban metis, encountered in St Louis or Dakar, would for the most part like to join in the life of the white minority, but they complain of being blocked by race prejudice. On the other hand, they criticize the blacks for what they consider their inadequate adjustment to the demands of modern life. Among the metis there is a recurrence of stereotypes already met with in the interviews with the French. Often the metis have a feeling of superiority towards the blacks while recognizing that the latter, in their life among themselves, evince a solidarity, a family spirit and a graciousness in personal relations of which the metis highly approve or to which at least they are very sensitive.

The most striking point noted is in the differing attitudes to the Africans on the one hand of the half-French metis, of whom the

St Louis metis are the prime example, and on the other of those who are half Senegalese and half Viet-Namese. For if the former feel torn between their fathers' and their mothers' communities, the latter are perfectly integrated into the national society of Senegal. This seems to us to show that the fact of being a metis does not in itself pose difficult problems of social integration. What really poses problems is cross-breeding between colonizers and colonized, because it introduces into the personalities of the offspring the conflicts arising from the former colonial situation.

The French-Senegalese metis are regarded by most Senegalese with some mistrust. They are accused of being conceited, or of wanting to stand apart from the African masses and of trying to merge with the European population. Here again we find the after-effects of the colonial situation.

Nevertheless, the relations between metis and Africans are not as tense as those between Africans and either Lebanese or French. The metis have mainly psychological problems, but in Senegal there is no socio-political metis problem. To the extent that they make their home in the country, they will sooner or later be integrated, that is to say Africanized.

Problems and prospects

Senegal is today an advanced national society. In other words, the black African ethnic groups of which it consists are thoroughly integrated into the collective life of the country. This is what is meant by saying that Senegal, in contrast with some other African countries, enjoys real ethnic harmony.

The fact remains that, while the sense of nationhood is widely shared in all *milieux,* the ethnic groups stand in different relationships to the combined society: the Wolof, Serer and Lébou are Senegalese pure and simple, while the Tukulor, Mandingo and Diola are geographically borderers and have cultural links with ethnic brothers outside Senegalese boundaries. The same is true of the Fulani and the small Bassari minority.

The peasant state which is that of the great bulk of the population, the fact that the great majority are also Muslims, and the absence of conflicts between people from the towns and people from the countryside, who have remained united by a multitude of bonds, all conduce to uniting the diversity of ethnic groups in a single nation. From this points of view, Senegal is exemplary. It is none the less desirable that the authorities should make some provision for the special cultural and linguistic needs of each ethnic group, more especially, the border groups. The maintenance of peace between the groups would be greatly assisted by the regionalized teaching of the country's various languages, allowing for the special place held by Wolof, and by economic redevelopment of the regions, according to their potential extra-territorial impact in a general West African framework. By this we mean that the national society of Senegal will have to attain its own final form and, at the same time, let down its barriers to a larger unity, without which no unrestricted development is likely to be possible. Thus a centralist Senegal would block the possibility of freedom in outward economic and cultural movement for the Tukulor, the Mandingo, the Diola and the Fulani, whereas a Senegal that was at once united and decentralized would enable these different ethnic groups to play a part towards the integration of Senegal, Mali and Guinea plus Gambia and Guinea-Bissao (once freed from Portuguese colonialism) in a West African totality. The gift of history of peace between ethnic groups should become a means of transcending the national context for the purpose of building Africa.

Be it added that Senegal is blessed with peace not only between ethnic groups but also between the Muslim majority and the Christian minority, not to mention the smaller minority still practising old traditional religions (the Diola and the Bassari, for example). However, one problem still subsists, notably among the Tukulor, the Fulani, the Mandingo and the Wolof, namely the question of caste. The rapid removal of the marriage prohibitions deriving from the former caste system and the general dissipation of caste prejudice would contribute greatly to the elimination, notably among the young, of both tensions and conflicts connected in this case with the survival of archaic ideas.

The African tradition of hospitality still honoured in Senegal should enable foreigners to live in peace with the indigenous population, though a prerequisite is that the foreigners should not be there as a controlling or specially privileged clique. Currently there are latent tensions between Lebanese and Senegalese, and overt tensions, capable of causing conflicts, are developing between

Senegalese and French. Among the Senegalese, the urban elements, and among the latter the most highly educated and often the youngest, are most acutely aware of these actual tensions and potential conflicts. In the face of the growing nationalism of the Senegalese, the colonialist, if not racialist, attitudes of some Lebanese or French take on the lineaments of ideological justification for the *status quo,* i.e. special privileges and exploitation. It is this which warrants the mention of inter-race tensions, although these tensions stem less from the racial differences of those concerned than from the economic and social dominance which the foreigners both enjoy and maintain. The Senegalization of responsible occupations and posts is clearly the perfect means of getting over these tensions and avoiding the development of conflicts. As regards the technical assistance that Senegal may need for a time, it would be advisable to internationalize it as quickly as possible.

In the final count, there are in Senegal no inter-ethnic tensions that are or may become obstacles to or brakes on development. The tensions between the Senegalese and the foreigners living in the country reflect the position of Senegal in relation to the foreign economic and political forces which hamper its development and compromise its independence. It may well be thought that the progress of the Senegalese community in the framework of a West African association requires that this position be changed in part or even in whole. In this respect, patriotism and African solidarity remain the motivations whereby the historic tasks of the hour can be accomplished.

Interviews with Wolof,
Serer, Tukulor, Fulani, Diola, Lébou, Mandingo
and some other ethnic groups

In the case of the interviews we carried out, we found that ethnic group membership was less important than religion. A Wolof or Tukulor will hesitate to give his daughter in marriage to a Diola, not so much because the man is a Diola as because many of the Diola are Roman Catholics.

The Wolof, since independence, have come to occupy many important positions in national life. All the same, the other ethnic groups very frequently consider the Wolof to be lazy, ambitious, dishonest, conceited, etc. There can be no denying that the other ethnic groups are becoming integrated in imitation of the Wolof, and yet ethnic groups like the Tukulor, the Diola and the Sarakolé still remain very much attached to their own cultural values, even though they live like the Wolof and speak the Wolof language.

It is interesting to note that a teasing kinship exists between the Tukulor, the Serer and the Diola. This kinship arises out of a 'blood compact' which gives it a sacred character. This form of kinship relation, while having a repressive side, embodies fellow-feeling and respect as well.

While members of the strictly African ethnic groups are less hostile towards one another, open hostility may be found towards the Lebanese, the Moors (Nar), Europeans and Cape Verde islanders. The metis are frequently viewed with a certain contempt.

Hostility towards the Lebanese is the most openly expressed. It must also be said that it is more often encountered than hostility towards other ethnic groups.

The attitude towards Europeans, called Toubab (particularly the French), still bears the imprint of colonial times. Tension exists beneath the surface because the European, after independence, instead of being one who assists, co-operates and maintains close relations with the native population, is still the 'foreigner', enjoying substantial material advantages without any sufficient justification.

On the other hand, the European, though considered a profiteer, is also accepted since in present circumstances it is impossible to do otherwise.

The Cape Verde islanders are criticized mainly for their liking for drink and for 'going on the spree'.

The metis are despised because they do not fall readily into any particular category. They are criticized mainly for taking sides with the Europeans rather than with the Africans.

Interview with Mr A

Mr A was 26, a Muslim Wolof, unmarried and a student. He considered the Wolof to be 'sociable, humane' and good practising Muslims.

According to Mr A, the Diola's situation has improved since independence. Before independence, the Diola had limited contacts with other people but are now more receptive, and one even finds Diola converted to the Muslim faith. The Diola are generally good-hearted but proud.

Mr A thought the Lébou all right, but behind the times. They are conservative and adopt modern ideas too slowly.

He considered the Serer hard-working but also too attached to their traditions.

Mr A described the Moors as racialist and sectarian and remarked that they do not like meeting Africans.

He told us that the Syrio-Lebanese were racialist as well but their racialism was of a concealed kind. All that mattered to them was profit. Mr A felt that

the racialism of the Syrio-Lebanese is much the same as that of the Europeans, who all the same have more to be said for them because they teach us a great deal. We owe the Europeans a lot. They are sociable and hard-working. The Europeans are all right in key posts because they know how to work and have the right qualifications for the work required of them.

What Mr A appreciated principally in Europeans was their attitude to work, their decency and the individualism of their way of life.

He very much regretted that 'Europeans are atheists'.

He expressed no ethnic preference with regard to the choice of his future wife.

Interview with Mr B

Mr B was 46, a Wolof and a Muslim by religion, like his three wives. He belonged to the Tidjaniya sect as did two of his wives while the third wife belonged to the Kadiriya sect. Mr B was a civil servant.

Speaking of the Wolof, Mr B thought that

a distinction has to be made between the Baol-Baol, the Dior-Dior (Cayorian), the Diam Bur-Diam Bur and the Djolof-Djolof because each of those groups has quite definite features differentiating it from the others.

A Baol-Baol will never let you know what he is thinking and always tries to worm secrets out of you. He is a good merchant and a good farmer. He is generally deceitful. The Baol-Baol are often Murrid Muslims.

The Dior-Dior (Cayorian) are good Muslims and also more open and more civilized than the others. They are almost all Tidjaniya Muslims.

The Diam Bur-Diam Bur are cheats [according to Mr B]. They never say what they are thinking or what they want to do. They are jealous, inquisitive and great traffickers.

As for the Djolof-Djolof, they are level-headed, thoughtful people. They are serious, practising Tidjaniya or Murrid Muslims. They are usually stock-breeders but are also successful as traders.

It should be noted that the Wolof in the large urban centres like Dakar, St Louis and Rufisque are descendants of the Djolof-Djolof, Baol-Baol and Dior-Dior and are more advanced than the rest. They spend their money almost as fast as they earn it because they want to live above their means and are continually being badgered by relations.

I do not know much about the Serer but I know they are sectarians, closely knit among themselves, and hard-working.

I know the Diola only from those who come to look for work in Dakar. I know that the girls who take jobs as maids work very hard.

The Lébou are just the same as they were fifty years ago. They have not progressed and they form a very tightly knit community. The Lébou representatives attached to the government, for example, will not sacrifice the interests of their community so as to get into the government's good books.

The Moors are successful retail traders. It must be said that they are here in Senegal only for their own interests.

I make no distinction between the Moor from Mauritania and the Senegalese Moor because the Moors call themselves Mauritanians even when they are black.

The Syrio-Lebanese, for their part, are merchants on a large scale who get rich very quickly. They help each other but do nothing disinterestedly. They do not even employ local labour. The Syrio-Lebanese are to be found in almost all branches of industry. I like them for sticking together but think it is deplorable that they should be here for their own interests alone. They do not like the native population. When they do employ local labour, they exploit the workers.

In my opinion, there can be no comradeship with Europeans. Europeans collaborate with people so long as they can make use of them. They collaborate when it is to their advantage to do so. As soon as there is nothing more to be got out of people, relations are allowed to drop. Europeans come to our countries because they are materially better off here. When they have to do with technical assistance, they make a lot of money, get themselves a good position and then go home. But as they never have enough, they try to stay on as long as they can.

Still, I like the way they behave, and admire them for knowing how to do things and how to manage their expenditure.

I have no particular feelings about the metis. I know, however, that the metis of St Louis used to think of themselves as Europeans, but things have changed. They are drawing closer to the other Senegalese. Prior to independence, a metis would not even say good-day to an African but now they think of themselves as being African, Senegalese, and particularly as coming from St Louis, because they think highly of the place.

The special position of the metis born of a Senegalese father and a European mother should be noted. He is closer to the Europeans because his mother, being European, has no contacts with African society. The children, in such cases, stand apart from African life and live like Europeans. They end up by thinking of themselves as Europeans.

The Cape Verde metis stick together and have little to do with anyone else. They live on the edge of Senegalese society, go in for pig-breeding and are excellent house-painters. They are sending their children more and more to French schools. The women generally work as maids or children's nannies for the Europeans. Some of them are employed as sales-girls in shops.

Interview with Mr C

Mr C was 40, a Wolof and a Muslim by religion like his wife.

The Wolof ethnic group is very important, especially in Senegal. The Wolof are intelligent, hospitable and sociable. I like the way they behave towards people from other ethnic groups. They have one remarkable quality, which is that they manage to absorb elements from other groups into their own, and the other ethnic groups are becoming more and more like the Wolof. The Wolof are very hospitable but not very nationalistic. It is true that all this is conducive to race mixture.

The Wolof joke a great deal. They are not so much restricted by family relationships as the Tukulor are.

There is a minority, a class among the Wolof, which can be seen to be trying to become Westernized, to be something different.

The Wolof regard themselves as a progressive ethnic group. They do not want the other ethnic groups to continue in existence. They bring about too many inter-ethnic marriages. The Wolof are not vindictive but they are provocative.

I think the Tukulor are very nationalistic. They are also very conservative. Whatever the Tukulor's social position, he likes to speak Tukulor and marries within his ethnic group. The Tukulor are a people who like to recall great events from their own history: El Hadj Omar, etc. Everything they do is inspired by the idea of keeping themselves in the Tukulor environment. Although sectarians, they are very sociable. They are also very thrifty. I don't think that my daughter could do better than choose a Tukulor as a husband. But I don't want my son to marry a Tukulor girl, because Tukulor women are too frivolous. They go with anyone. A Tukulor woman doesn't get to know anyone until after her marriage. I am not in favour of a marriage like that. The Tukulor are hard-working chaps, though, who set great store by kinship. A Tukulor's house is open to the whole Tukulor community. The Tukulor do not want anyone from another ethnic group to join the Tukulor circle.

I think the Tukulor marry too early. They pay no attention to age differences between marriage partners. It is not uncommon to see a 50-year-old man marrying a 14-year-old girl. That is why the girl has to go and take lovers here, there and everywhere. That is the Tukulor girl's great misfortune.

The Serer are difficult to judge because they fall into several groups. I know that the Serer from the Sine claim a more honourable status than the other Serer and also than the other ethnic groups. They consider themselves to be the most important ethnic group. I should not object if my daughter wanted to marry a Serer because the Serer know how to be happy with what they've got.

I think the Diola are all right; they are energetic chaps who maintain the primacy of their ethnic group. They are conservative and prefer to marry within their ethnic group.

Diola women do not take account of the man's social position in choosing a husband and they have a community spirit. The Diola are as nationalistic as the Tukulor. They are energetic and very hard-working. They always keep in touch with the place they come from because they look after the work of the fields during the winter season. They are the ethnic group which allows the greatest economic progress. The Diola are competitive. Every time there is a competition or other examination, you know, the Diola take the top places.

I should like my son to marry a Diola woman because Diola women are thrifty. They manage not to spend too much.

The Lébou are a proud lot and sectarian. And yet they are an ethnic group that is tending to split up. They have changed and as they make progress, they are living a little outside their territory. They like joining with other ethnic groups. They used to be a closed ethnic group but are now opening up, which makes marriage possible with members of other ethnic groups.

The Lébou have lost all they used to possess. They used to be great landowners.

The Lébou are not very sociable. They are also too devout. They are clannish and very conservative. They still have theocratic power.

Long before independence, some of the power was in the hands of the Lébou and some in the hands of the Wolof.

The Lébou are very intelligent. Although they are conservative, it is to be noted that they have abandoned certain rites that they used to celebrate once upon a time.

Generally speaking, the Nar are great sectarians. The Nar Ganar do not give much away. The only relations they have with other ethnic groups are those of trade. They sell and we buy. They don't get married but they run after the girls. The Nar are good, practising Muslims and also very thrifty. All that matters as far as they are concerned, is getting money. However much a Nar may own, he will always sleep on a mat. They always live below the level their means would allow whereas the Serer and the Diola live according to their means. The Nar won't have anything to do with modern life.

The black Nar are 'Wolofized' and like everything the Wolof do except where clothes are concerned. The Nar are rather backward and it is uncommon to find any of them in an enviable situation.

My daughter will not marry a Nar because they do not have the same ideas as we do. They reject modernity and are, at best, merchants or butchers.

The Syrio-Lebanese are a great affliction. They are exploiters. They come to exploit us. They really do nothing else. I think they shouldn't even be included among those who are on friendly terms with us. When they make friends, it is solely in their own interest. The relations between us are purely commercial. You do not often find a Lebanese man marrying a Senegalese girl and it is just as uncommon to see a Lebanese girl marrying a Senegalese man.

I would not let my daughter marry a Syrio-Lebanese because they do not have the same customs as we do.

The Toubab was in the country as an exploiter and he has remained the same. Toubabs help you only when they want something. There are strings attached to any help they give. A Toubab never does anything for nothing. Even when a European marries an African, it is not for ever. I am not in favour of Europeans. Progress doesn't require anything other than professional relations with them. Once the Toubab can no longer exploit the country he will leave. They are intelligent people, very intelligent, who know how to make use of others. It has to be admitted that they are the cleverest people in the world. The Syrio-Lebanese are not so clever. The European manages to exploit us without its being obvious.

I would not let my daughter marry a European.

The metis have contacts with everyone. They hang together. They are exemplary workers and there are not many metis in poor jobs.

I chose a Wolof wife who is related to me and whom my parents wanted me to marry. The important thing in marriage, in my opinion, is first of all love, the parents' views and after that, the means available for getting married.

Interview with Mr F

Mr F was 31 years old and a Wolof like his wife. Both were Tidjaniya Muslims. He had studied political science and is now in business.

The Wolof are an ethnic group which tends to colonize the rest. They are, nevertheless, the link between the various ethnic groups. The Wolof are very conceited, due to the fact that there are more of them in public life than there are people from other ethnic groups. It should also be mentioned that the Wolof language is the principal language of communication.

The Lébou are a rather closed group. They are very proud of themselves and I should not object if my daughter wanted to marry a Lébou. What matters in marriage is mutual love.

The Tukulor are willing and hard working. They never refuse to take on anything. You find Tukulor at all levels in various jobs. The main thing is that they are very resourceful. They are more willing than the Wolof but there are greater differences among them. By that, I mean that the Tukulor differ from region to region. If joint action is called for, the Wolof are more go-ahead and efficient than the Tukulor. The Tukulor is proud of his village first and his region next. You find the same sort of thing among the Baol-Baol, the Saloum-Saloum, the people from St Louis and the Cayorian.

The Wolof is more resourceful than the others. He can take advantage of opportunities.

I do not know much about the Diola. There seems to me to be something paradoxical about them. I was surprised by the relations existing between men and women in Casamance. It was the women who mostly went out to work, at least in the few families I visited. The man's job was to look after the children and I wondered who was in charge in the home.

The Diola have remained apart, in a primitive state. They are becoming more and more up to date since they have started moving to the big centres.

I know that the Sarakolé and the Mandingo are hard workers and make up 95 per cent of the African workers in France.

I know that the Serer have been proud since independence because the president of the republic is a Serer. But the Tukulor were also proud in the days of Mamadou Dia.

The Mauritanian Nar are lazy but very sharp traders. They are lazy over any work which requires effort. They are opportunists in business. They manage to unite to defend their interests, and you don't find that among the others.

My daughter could marry a Nar if she wanted to.

The Syrio-Lebanese come here to exploit us. They are exploiters. They don't let slip any chance to make something out of the business they are engaged in here. The only proof I need is the way they support what the President of the Republic does and the way they have joined the UPS,[1] which enables them to protect their business interests even better. They are not interested in developing trade in Senegal; they are just feathering their own nests. They send abroad 150 per cent of what they earn in their business and the government helps them. I would be against my daughter's marrying a Syrio-Lebanese because I don't like them. I don't like the way they go on or the way they work in our country.

There are some Frenchmen, you know, whom I admire and who try to do something for the country. But there are others who take advantage of the country. I have never seen one Syrio-Lebanese trying to do anything for Senegal.

1. Union Progressiste Sénégalaise.

I am not in favour of Europeans being systematically sent home. They're here to earn their living like everyone else. I'm in favour of keeping those who work honestly, but there are some whom I'd willingly kill off.

They still have a feeling of superiority dating from the colonial period. There are prejudices of which they can't manage to rid themselves.

I'm against mixed marriages because they create a tremendous number of social problems, because habits and customs aren't the same.

Interview with Mr G

Mr G was 40 years old. He was married to a cousin and, like her, was a Tukulor. Both were Muslims. Mr G was a civil servant.

I voluntarily chose my wife from within the family. I knew of marriages breaking down between couples from different families. I thus made the marriage of my own choice. I was not in favour of long-haired women [Europeans] coming here. You can go out with them in Europe but not bring them back home. Since we have to go back to our families, one might just as well choose a wife from within the family.

If I had to get married again, I would at least marry a Tukulor woman if I couldn't find a wife in my own family, because we would get on better together.

I don't have much faith in Wolof women because they are too sophisticated. They are independent and they like big head-scarves. I think the woman's place is in the home and I can only find the sort of woman I want within my ethnic group.

Besides that, my name carries a lot of weight in my ethnic group. I'm somebody. Inside your ethnic group, you can think of marrying any kind of woman but your choice is automatically limited in other ethnic groups. Each ethnic group defends itself. For example, when a Wolof comes to us to look for a wife, we give him the riff-raff, you know, the unmarried mothers and the daughters of our slaves. I am very conservative and a Muslim.

I have social relationships with Tukulor mostly through force of circumstances. I live in this circle, I go to the family ceremonies of other people just as they show an interest in these same problems when they concern me. That doesn't mean that I have no contacts with members of other ethnic groups, however. I have contacts even with the Toubab. I loathe receptions, though, because people have to go wearing a dark suit. I'm fond of wearing my caftan and my boubou. I don't see what respectability has to do with what you wear.

I have no daughter as yet. I do have to arrange the marriages of daughters of relations, however. If one of these girls wanted to marry someone from another ethnic group one day, I would advise her against it because the fact of going to live away from her own people means taking risks. I would say to her: 'If you marry this man we shan't know if you are unhappy and we shan't be able to help you. And then once you go outside your husband's house, you won't be able to turn to anyone.' All the same, I'd do nothing to prevent such a marriage if the Diola or the Serer can keep the girl. I should just warn her about the risks and uncertainties of marrying into another ethnic group.

If there was any difference in living standard, I would prevent the marriage. That's already happened, anyway.

In choosing a wife, I like to marry within my ethnic group but I am not in favour of too close a consanguinity. I married a cousin six times removed. She's from my family without being so in fact.

If I can't marry so as to avoid close consanguinity, I prefer to find a wife from within my ethnic group. I think that a couple should have something in common and that they should be linked by belonging to the same ethnic group.

I think the Diola are obedient people; they don't shirk work and they seem to me to behave well. They're easy to get on with. You always have to tell a Diola what to do. You mustn't put him in charge or give him much responsibility. When you take one of the rank and file and put him in charge it doesn't work.

The Serer are cousins and we really belong to the same ethnic group. They are quite harmless, really. They don't face up to work so well as the Diola. They're cleverer than the Diola. They're more energetic in action, but they remain mysterious all the same: Serer from the Sine, Serer from the Saloum, it's not very clear, the distinction isn't very clear-cut. I'd be more inclined to marry a Muslim Serer woman than a Muslim Wolof woman.

The Wolof are a big-mouthed lot, always ready with complaints but not prepared to stick to their guns. You must never get involved in a row with them because they leave you to face the music all alone afterwards. They always manage to get off scot-free.

The Lébou are good chaps. They are fishermen. All the same, they are difficult to get on with. They often stir up trouble for the Tukulor. There was an incident at N'Gor as a result of which all the Tukulor living there moved out. There were a large number of Tukulor there who were mostly employed as waiters or cooks in the various restaurants of the district. One of these was making up to a Lébou woman and it got known and degenerated into a fight between the two ethnic groups.

Lébou husbands are very jealous but their women have very easy-going morals. It's true that all women in towns are easy-going. They let themselves be tempted by money, and anyway, you have to admit that morals tend to get lax in towns.

There have been groups whose social and economic situation has improved since independence. The Wolof's situation has steadily improved. The other ethnic groups haven't done so well. The Diola's situation hadn't improved before now because they were in opposition.

The Tukulor have managed to reap some small advantages but they have not been of much use to them because they are a group lacking in cohesion, where dissent is a permanent feature. The leaders are being challenged by the rank and file.

The regions where the Wolof live have had the benefit of considerable capital investment. But they are also the ones in which misappropriation and embezzlement of public funds are rife. The Wolof don't even regard embezzlement as dishonourable any more, but it's different with the Tukulor. The Wolofs are the ones who have got the most out of independence. The head of State is a Serer but this has been of no advantage to the Serer. The Bambara-Malinké group looked for a while as if they were reaping considerable benefits from independence. There was the break-up of Mali, after which Eastern Senegal also had its share of the post-independence economic advantages, like a shock wave.

The people from Dahomey and Togo have made nothing out of it, but they find a peaceful atmosphere in which to work in Senegal.

The Fulani from Guinea are free to set up in businesses in Senegal and are free not to be active in a political party.

I think the Syrio-Lebanese are crooks. They always contrive to exploit the population. They are the ones who lend money to everyone and make substantial profits out of it. They are very successful in business.

You can't call them racialist but they exploit the blacks. They are crafty. Wherever their interests are at stake, nationality is no obstacle. They'll run with the hare and hunt with the hounds.

Sékou Touré is the man who's found the answer to the Syrio-Lebanese problem. In fact, to be in business in Guinea you have to be of Guinean nationality, once and for all. You are Guinean and you stay in Guinea. There's no question of dual nationality as there is here.

The Mauritanian Moors or Mauritanian Nar are a running sore. They're racialist, they don't like the blacks and they get hold of the very small businesses which ought to be kept for the Senegalese.

The Nar are no use here. They ought to go back to their *ganar* country] where the blacks are downtrodden. The Nar don't deserve to be treated as we treat them here.

The Senegalese Nar, in so far as he is Senegalese, speaks the languages of the ethnic group with which he lives. He makes it clear as often as is necessary that he is not a Nar from Mauritania.

There ought to be migration controls on these foreign Nar from Mauritania. There ought to be regulations about their getting work here, too. Mauritanian law protects the Moors quite well and not the blacks. Something ought to be done here to protect the blacks.

Where the metis are concerned, you have to distinguish between the metis from St Louis, the Senegal-Moroccan, the Cape Verde, and the recent Franco-African metis.

The St Louis metis or Goumettes are said to have terrible complexes. They generally look down on their mothers.

The Senegal-Moroccan metis are a bit better adapted to society than the St Louis metis. There is a Muslim middle class of which they represent the summit. They are really descended, more or less, from Sheik Hamet Tidiane. They say they are sherifs.

Whenever a girl has a Moroccan father, she marries one of her cousins.

The European-Senegalese metis have a complex and feel the strain of their position more. They used to consider themselves the equals of the whites or only just a little inferior. They prefer to marry among themselves or to marry Europeans.

The Cape Verde islanders are a hotbed of disease. The women have very loose morals and breed like flies. They have no racial antipathies so far as townsfolk are concerned. There are all kinds of metis. You find Cape Verde mothers whose children have Wolof, Serer, Diola, etc. fathers but not the other way round. You don't find a Cape Verde man with a wife from another Senegalese people.

There is very great sexual freedom in this group. It is true that they are poor folk and that promiscuity plays a considerable part in this sexual freedom.

They are good hairdressers and good shoemakers. They are industrious and much appreciated. But the Wolof and the Serer criticize them for drinking too much and for eating pork.

The metis who have come from France are still growing up and one can see that they live in an enclosed environment. Former African students who have married European wives are friendly with each other. They must be allowed time to settle in before they can be judged.

What is already plain is that all the ethnic groups show signs of rejecting this class of metis.

Muslim Africans regard mixed African-European marriages as wrong in two ways. It is wrong for the African to marry a European if he can't manage to lead his wife along the straight and narrow path of religion and may even let himself be led astray by her. It is also wrong, but politically wrong this time, because the European women married to Africans are foreigners who intend to remain as such and this perpetuates a complex towards the Europeans.

I have a lot of friends who have married European wives and we haven't seen each other since they got married.

Once an African has married a Frenchwoman, he finds many of his problems solved, such as getting a job and finding somewhere to live. Apart from this injustice perpetuated out of a mistaken sense of fellowship, there is nothing else to be said for the time being. This pressure group is going too far. How is this little society, which is being closely watched by the native society, going to develop?

Interview with Mr H

Mr H was 40 years old, a Muslim Tukulor employed in the Post Office.

I have had three successive wives. The first one was a Wolof, the second a Tukulor-Wolof metis and the third a Tukulor. I don't know what the fourth one will be. I have no preference for any particular ethnic group. It all depends on whether the girl pleases me.

The Wolof are practical people who have their feet firmly on the ground. They are very much concerned with their material interests. They are inclined to sacrifice everything for the satisfaction of their material interests and this makes it possible for them to live on good terms with everyone.

I criticize them for not paying enough attention to the higher things in life and for not taking a clear stand on important issues like politics, ethics and religion. I would agree to my daughter's marrying a Wolof because the main thing is that the man should be the sort she likes.

The Tukulor are decent folk. Tukulor society is rather breaking up, you know, because the Tukulor are increasingly losing their society's cultural and moral values. The Tukulor used to be a very good fellow who cared for his dignity, his religion, his family and his country. He was also considerate towards the other races [ethnic groups]. Unfortunately, all that is gradually going. It's only the good families which keep these principles intact.

I don't know much about the Lébou. In spite of having lived with the colonizers for a long time, they are, I think, a people who have not retained much of the colonizers' culture. I feel they are people who have stayed rather primitive.

My daughter can marry a Lébou if she wishes.

The Serer are the Tukulor's slaves. The Serer are Tukulor who fled from the River region when faced with the threat of Islamization. We are cousins and that's why I call them 'slaves'. In fact, they are people who have remained very pure. They are kind and straightforward especially towards the Tukulor.

I know the Diola to be hard-working. They are very simple people but their family organization is similar to that of the Europeans [individualism]. With them, it's 'every man for himself and God for everyone'. I wonder whether this state of affairs may not have been due to the White Fathers who were successful among this ethnic group.

I don't like European-African metis (born of a European father and an African mother) because I don't know of a single metis who is a decent sort. They are people you cannot rely on. They oscillate between two races and always incline towards the stronger side. In a word, they are opportunists.

I've just remembered that I do know a decent metis, after all, from Arboussier, but even in his case religion separates us. There's no question of my allowing my daughter to marry a metis.

The Arab-Senegalese metis have the same religion as myself. They fit more easily into their mother's background. Even when they are well off, they live more or less as we do. They might even like to be completely absorbed. There are very few who have gone back to their father's country. I could let my daughter marry one of these metis because religion is an important factor.

The Nana Cape Verde islanders are a degenerate lot, always ill. They have syphilis and varicose veins; they drink and they're dirty. You can't have anything to do with those people.

The Wolof are a very practical people. They have always been able to come to terms with the government and have had a better time since independence. There isn't a single Tukulor in the present government,[1] although the Tukulor are the ethnic group with the most high-grade personnel in Senegal. The River region hasn't anything else to export but its children's brains.

The Wolof are the ones who've made most out of independence. They are very practical. Even in their human relations. When you are courting a Wolof woman, she gives you big smiles to get all she can out of you.

I know the Mauritanian Nar well because I did my Koranic studies among them. We are neighbours and I speak Moorish. People often have false ideas about the Moors. The Moors in Senegal aren't the same as the

1. It may be mentioned that this statement is not correct.

Moors in Mauritania. They come here to make money and when they have got enough they go. They avoid social contacts, they avoid living expensively, and they don't bring their wives here. They are very likeable people in their own country, provided that they find you share the same traditional values.

I would not willingly let my daughter marry a Moor because she would go a long way away. I would happily marry a Moorish woman, though preferably an educated one. I can't say as much for the other races. The Portuguese are people without any tradition and then there aren't any healthy Portuguese women.[1]

You must also distinguish the Moorish captives or slaves, most of whom are Tukulor. They remain slaves. They are better off in Senegal than in Mauritania. They marry among themselves or marry Tukulor slaves.

You can't lump all Europeans together. There are the ones who live in Europe, the ones connected with colonization and the post-independence ones. There are cultivated Europeans and then you have the poor whites. There is the man who really wants to co-operate and the one who has come to make money; there is the open-minded European and the one who's the reverse.

The Europeans of the colonial period aren't worth anything, they're nothing, it's not worth even talking about them.

The post-independence Europeans have come to co-operate, but at the present time there aren't any sincere co-operators. There are people running away from the difficulties of European life, who come here to make money. The poor white is the grocer, the salesman, the mechanic and the trader. They're not worth anything either, because they are people who think themselves superior and go on looking down on people as happened during the colonial era.

And it must be said that some of the co-operators are humbugs, like the man, all smiles, who's a technical adviser somewhere. He says he knows Africa. Have you ever seen an African live in France for twenty years without speaking French and without going to a Frenchman's home, etc? Well, that's the way the co-operators behave here. Then they go and set themselves up as technical advisers who know what pleases and interests the Africans better than the Africans themselves. Nothing is done here unless the Europeans do it and they manage so well that the Senegalese don't want anything to do with any of it.

You mustn't even rely on the Frenchman who just wants to come to Africa. He only has to set foot here to have all his good intentions altered.

1. This refers to blacks or metis from countries under Portuguese domination.

There's no question of my daughter's marrying a European. Personally I shall never marry a European woman. If one of my relations marries one, I cut him out of my life.

Interview with Mr J

Mr J was 39. He was a Tidjaniya Muslim, a Fulani who had married a Lébou. He was in business.

It is just by chance that my wife belongs to the Lébou ethnic group. I didn't have any particular preference for any special ethnic group. I have no tribal sense and I have not given any thought to the question of what differences there may be between the ethnic groups.

Here, everybody is Wolof to a greater or lesser extent. All I know is that the Wolof are tall and light in colour.

The Tukulor are too regionalistic. They are very attached to the Muslim faith. There are jobs which are restricted to them alone, for example, shoe-cleaners and waiters. You get the feeling that these jobs are hereditary. They are very much attached to their traditions. This is surely due to the fact that they have had great men like El Hadj Omar in their history.

I have noticed that the ethnic groups from which great men have come never forget what these men did in the past. When you speak about El Hadj Omar to the Tukulor, you give them the feeling of being superior to everybody else.

The Lébou are our wives [Mr J refers to his wife in this way. In marrying a Lébou woman, he has married the Lébou ethnic group]. We are accustomed to chaff them by saying that they are not very gifted. Without being unpleasant, you can say that they certainly are backward but they are nervertheless very hardy folk, like all seafarers. The Guet N'Dar people at St Louis are a bit like the Bretons, used to a hard life. I won't object if my daughter wants to marry a Lébou one day.

The Serer are *gamou*.[1] They are mostly Christians. They also go in for the traditional religions and, when they are Muslims, they are not very good ones. Even if they are converted to Islam they do not give up the traditional practices. Incidentally, others go in for those traditional practices as well, but not as much as the Serer.

The Serer are very conservative.

I don't make any distinction between a Diola and a Mandiac. The ones I know are very likeable. I have the feeling that the Diola tend to be Muslims. I believe they are good marabouts as well. In fact I'm not too

1. *Gamou*: teasing kinsfolk.

ure about what I'm saying, as I told you I don't know what the difference
s between the Diola and the Mandiac.

The Fulani are tall, handsome and proud. They are very much
attached to their traditions. They are shy and like to keep themselves to
themselves too much.

I like the Nar from Mauritania—but only in their own country. They
adapt remarkably easily and this means they get hold of all the small
businesses. The Nar know how to make do with a little. They hoard up
their money, so that they bleed the country of money which they take
back to Mauritania.

I would let my daughter marry a Nar because I feel he is an African
just like the rest and he could make my daughter happy. It's not the race
or the ethnic group which matters.

I don't know very much about the Senegalese Nar or black Mauritanian Nar. I know they are slaves or descendants of slaves who just seem
to be content with their lot.

The Syrio-Lebanese are a running sore in this country. A very large
slice of the business cake is in their hands and it ought to belong to the
Senegalese. With very few exceptions they are neither a caste nor a class.
They very readily intermarry with other ethnic groups.

The metis, except those from St Louis, aren't used to being metis.
They feel inferior to the white race. Their daughters go more for European
men and their sons for European girls.

The ordinary man approaches them as he would approach a European simply because they behave like Europeans.

A metis from St Louis would never ask to marry my daughter but if
he did, I wouldn't say no.

The new Cape Verde metis are proud of being what they are. The old
ones have become a part of the Senegalese people. The men remain
attached to their ethnic group but the women marry people who are not
from Cape Verde and abandon their race.

The metis born of a Cape Verde mother and a Senegalese father
behave like Senegalese since their mother becomes Senegalese. A Portuguese woman who marries a Senegalese does not live among her own
people any more. The Cape Verde women even speak Wolof among
themselves sometimes.

I like the Europeans, but in their own country; by extension,
Europeans means the French as far as we are concerned. I am not racialistic
but, so far as I am concerned, the French are identified with the colonial
history of France and it's a fact that, though we are independent, they are
still holding all the key posts in the country, particularly in economic
affairs.

Unlike the Syrio-Lebanese, they regularly make use of a lot o
Africans, but all the same, they stop able Africans from setting up i
business in certain lines.

They are much less arrogant than they were. You find some who are
very nice and very reasonable but it's not written on their faces that the
are like this. So we are forced to carry on the struggle we want for ou
economic independence everywhere. This independence must necessaril
take the form of transferring their economic power to the Senegalese
There is no shortage of Senegalese to take control of the country's eco
nomic future.

Apart from private life, when you come into the political field, thos
who are there, the technical-assistance people, only look after the interest
of France and not the interests of our country. Officially, though, they ar
there to help us to discover what is in our interests.

I would oppose my daughter's marrying a European with all m
strength because, first, the colonial period is still too recent, and, second
because the recent metis look down on the blacks. My grandchildre
would be liable to look down on us. All the same, 'look down on' isn'
the right expression. It would be better to say that they would not sho
me any consideration.

I have very good friends in France, they had some very good qualities
But here, I haven't any Toubab friends; you're obliged to generalize an
so to adopt a hard-and-fast attitude, which is even sometimes unjus
towards some of them. We don't try to make any distinction between th
good ones and the bad.

I reject them as a whole in the context of the relations between us

Interview with Mr K

Mr K was 32. He was a Tidjaniya Muslim Tukulor, a civil servan
married to a Wolof woman.

To begin with, you don't want to mix with other races but you're alway
travelling; I met my wife, I liked her and we got married. I don't mak
any distinction between the races.

The Wolof are no different from the other ethnic groups. You mee
people among them—as you do everywhere—who are difficult to get o
with and others who are less difficult. My relations with the Wolof ar
with my parents-in-law: they are polite and kindly.

I don't know much about the Serer. I can see that the Serer girl
employed as maids are very hard-working. They put up with being tol
what to do in order to earn their living.

I don't know anything at all about the Diola. I might know a little about the Serer but I know nothing about the Diola.

The Tukulor are nice but they don't like being told what to do. They always want to be in the right. There is a teasing kinship between the Wolof and the Tukulor.[1] Most of the Tukulor are farmers but there are also a lot of intellectuals. I criticize them for sending their little children into the street as Bana-Bana [illicit child street vendors], little bandits who are picked up by the police and put in prison.

When the Tukulor works, he prefers to take everything he earns back home with him to his village. They want to have everything at home. Do you know, at the moment I am being criticized because I have a house in Cape Verde instead of in the Fouta. They say you ought to have a house in Cape Verde but another one as well in the Fouta in case you lose your job in Cape Verde.

The Fulani are herdsmen who don't live in villages. They stay in the bush to guard the herd, being very attached to it. They only use an animal for meat when it is in very poor health. They're never well-dressed. In any case, they can't be clean because they are always following the cows.

The Lébou are fishermen.

The Sarakolé generally work on the steamers. They are also technicians and great travellers.

They are the richest of all the ethnic groups. They have to bring back money or perish in the attempt, that's all they live for.

The Mauritanian Nar are too much like the Algerians. They are mostly small-bazaar merchants. They are very thrifty. A Nar begins by selling water and then, a little later, you see him in a small shop. They try to belittle the blacks by the language they use, calling them slaves.

The Syrio-Lebanese are businessmen. They know how to work together and how to get rich by selling on credit. The young Syrio-Lebanese think they own the city of Dakar. I don't know whether they are allowed to, but they create havoc in the traffic with their mopeds. They ought to behave better so as to leave people in peace. Do you know, at Avenue Gambetta for example, they cross the street just any old how and you're the one who has to put your brakes on. They let off firecrackers in the cinemas. They are the bourgeoisie of the town, of course. All the money in Senegal flows into their pockets. They've got beautiful houses, lovely cars and all the business is in their hands.

The Europeans are the people who taught us French. They aren't very racialist people. Some are, some aren't. They know how to collaborate. There are some who make trouble and do the black man down. Nevertheless, they feel they have to help people. Most Europeans can't

1. Untrue.

see someone in trouble without trying to help him. Some are open-minded and always want to help. Those people are prepared to do anything for somebody who has nothing. There are good and bad, as there are in any ethnic group.

I would not let my daughter marry a European because of the differences between their standard of living and ours. If I could afford to, I would marry a European woman but as I am just an ordinary chap, I'm not going to marry one.

The metis are practically like the Nar. They are people who look down on the blacks although they are neither black nor white.

The Portuguese are mostly painters. I don't know them.

Interview with Mr O

Mr O was 50 years old. He was a Serer, a Roman Catholic by religion, married to a Gambian woman. Mr O worked as a storekeeper.

I got married to my wife rather by chance.

As the moment, there are two big ethnic groups on the up and up. There are the Serer and the Tukulor. Those are perhaps the ones I know most about.

The Serer are very proud of being Serer. They have become aware of it since independence. Many Serer have reached an educational level unthinkable ten years ago. I also know that at the moment they are busy regrouping in an attempt to take on the whole Serer ethnic group. I've seen philosophers and sociologists getting together in order to find out more about this ethnic group.

They are honest folk. They tend to be open-minded and receptive too, at the present time. They used to be closed in on themselves. The young people today are trying to marry people from outside their ethnic group but their parents are still conservative and make difficulties. You can see that they are opening up, all the same.

The faults are with the women, who don't help their husbands very much. The women are very attached to their religion but that doesn't stop them keeping up some traditional practices.

The Wolof are in a rather special position because you can't say that they are a clear-cut ethnic group. They always overlap with several other ethnic groups. They have a lot of faults: they are spendthrifts; they haven't got much family feeling. The most dishonest people are among the Wolof. They are very proud and think they are superior to the other big ethnic groups: for the life of me I can't see why.

If my daughter wanted to marry a Wolof, I would give her advice but I couldn't stop her because she's the one who's getting married.

should try to find out if the man concerned could support my daughter. The religious side interests me very little.

The Tukulor are hard-working and proud of their race. They like improving themselves and finding things out. They think a lot of their customs and respect their leaders. They have a strong family feeling. They have one small fault, which is that they are self-centred. The Tukulor comes before all the other ethnic groups.

I would let my daughter marry a Tukulor.

I don't know much about the Lébou but I think they are like the Serer. What is certain, is that the Lébou knows only the Lébou. But I don't think that, even among themselves, they get on particularly well.

I wouldn't let my daughter marry a Lébou because I don't see anything in them which could attract me.

I don't know very much about the Diola. I don't know what I'd do if a Diola wanted to marry my daughter, because I don't know them.

I can't stand the Nar at any price. If there's one race I don't like it's them. I think they're too mean. They don't like the other Senegalese ethnic groups. They're here for their business and that's all. If I had anything to do with it, they wouldn't still be here.

I would be against my daughter's marrying a Nar.

I'd put the Lebanese in the same category as the Nar. They are exactly the same. My daughter won't marry a Lebanese.

The Cape Verde islanders are just like the Nar and I wouldn't let my daughter marry one of them either.

There are some metis who are all right and who think of themselves as real Senegalese. Those people are all right but there are very few of them. Three-quarters of them try to be like the Toubab. The Toubab are even closer to the Senegalese than they are. While the Toubab are pleased to associate with Senegalese, the metis avoid doing so.

I wouldn't let my daughter marry a metis because I know that it wouldn't last.

I've got real friends among the Europeans. I had one friend who was like a brother to me. My problems were his and his problems were mine. He left six months ago and we write to each other every week. There aren't many like him. I wouldn't hesitate to let my daughter marry a European of that sort.

I think that technical-assistance people have to be here to help with medicine. I can't understand why they are needed in teaching because there are Senegalese, even in higher education. They could be replaced by Senegalese or Africans. There's no point in having them here in business.

What matters in choosing a wife is the way she behaves: she must be able to keep house, look after the children and see to their school work.

Interview with Mr S

Mr S was 24 years old. He was a Baynouk,[1] a Muslim by religion, unmarried and worked as a storekeeper.

I've no particular preference as regards the choice of a wife. I'll even go further and say I've no particular preference for any race.

I've not had any contact with my ethnic group. It's tending to become absorbed into the Diola and Mandingo ethnic groups. They're very open-minded and receptive. I've discovered indeed that it's this openness which has led to their being despoiled, in the end, of everything they possessed by the people they received with open arms.

They're rebellious and are always challenging the established order. My father is listened to by a great number of them. The government has had its way over rice-growing but the Baynouk are still complaining about it.

The Diola have taken over my ancestors' land. That's the only thing I have against them. I have to admit that they're very hard-working, especially the Diola women. I'd let my daughter marry a Diola, certainly, but she'll be able to choose her husband quite freely.

I've got no complaints about the Wolof. I find them very quick-witted. I criticize the young people I go around with for being too cheeky.

I'd let my daughter marry a Wolof, and even a Toubab, if she wanted to.

I don't know much about the Tukulor but I get on very well with the ones I'm friendly with.

My best friend is a Lébou, so you can judge from that.

The Cape Verde islanders are too keen on living together. They aren't exactly noted for their cleanliness. They used to form little groups on their own at first but now they join up with others.

I don't have anything to do with the Moors. I don't know anything about them except that they have always been reputed to be dirty.

I think the Lebanese monopolize our economy without creating any opportunities. They don't take on Senegalese workers, they do everything themselves and don't do anything effective to bring Senegal out of a state of underdevelopment.

I knew a student who had been educated here and he considered himself Senegalese, but every time there was a strike, he would dissociate himself from the Senegalese. When he finished his studies, he quickly went back to the Lebanon. The Lebanese are confounded opportunists.

I work in a place where there are a large number of technical-assistance people. You have to distinguish between three kinds: those

1. A small ethnic group from Lower Casamance, going back further in origin than the Diola.

who want to help Senegal; those who are trying to line their pockets; and the neo-colonialists.

They're a serious obstacle to our emancipation.

I wouldn't like to be a metis. It's not because they are ill-treated but I don't like half measures. The metis, in general, suffer from complexes. They feel they are Toubab. Others want to prove they are Negroes and they overdo it. I saw one of my teachers who was a metis have a fight with the headmaster who criticized him for not being a native, and then he started to cry. It was pitiful.

Interview with Miss X

Miss X was 17. She was a Diola Muslim working as a nurserymaid.

I shall choose a Muslim as my future husband. The Diola are all right. They're nice. I like the Diola because I am a Diola.

The Wolof aren't nice. They lie. They're thieves. They're vulgar. There are Wolof who are nice, though.

The Lébou are the same as the Wolof. But the Wolof throw their clothes off when they dance and that's bad.

I shouldn't let my daughter marry a Wolof because she'd be insulted by him if they had an argument and I don't like that.

The Lébou is just the same. There are only the Lébou and the Wolof that I wouldn't let my daughter marry.

The Serer aren't like the Wolof; they're nice, those people.

The Tukulor are nice, they say their prayers properly and know all about God.

The Nar are all right here but they're not nice in their own country. If you go to their country, they beat you and call you a black. Here they're nice because they need to carry on their business. Apart from that, they're good Muslims; they pray a lot.

I don't know anything about the Lebanese.

The Portuguese drink too much. They don't say their prayers. I wouldn't let my daughter marry a Portuguese because they don't know about God.

The metis are in the middle. If the metis is born of a black mother and a white father, that isn't good. Black should marry black and white, white.

The Toubab are all right because they work a lot and don't steal like the Africans. They don't know about God and say that God does not exist.

I shan't let my daughter marry a Toubab because they're not Muslim.

Interview with Mr Y

Mr Y was 43 years old. He had two wives, who were Lébou like himself. Mr Y worked as a chauffeur.

I'm a Lébou and I prefer to have two wives who are Lébou like myself. As far as I'm concerned, the Lébou, the Wolof and the Serer are the same and I make no distinction between them. There are lots of Diola who are nice but some of them are unpleasant. Nowadays, they're educated, civilized and nicer. In the old days, they wouldn't have any non-Diola among them. They weren't like us.

The Tukulor are all right, but I don't know much about them as I haven't lived with the Tukulor.

The Mauritanian Nar I see are all right.

I don't know the Lebanese. I just go to their shops, that's all.

I know there are some metis who are nice but there are some who are very unpleasant as well.

There are some nice Toubab and there are some who aren't nice.

Interview with Mr G

Mr G was 51. He was a Muslim Sarakolé of the Kadiriya sect. He was married, with three wives, two of whom were Lébou and one Baol-Baol.

The Sarakolé are very clean and dignified. They are kind and are good Muslims. They are very talkative, but they aren't ill-natured. They also stick together.

I was born in Senegal where there aren't many Sarakolé women. That's the reason I didn't marry one.

The Wolof are very good chaps because they're patient like the Sarakolé. They're crafty and are crafty with everybody. They think themselves craftier than anybody else. They always want to be up above the others [superior to other people]. I would let my daughter marry a Wolof.

The Lébou are the people . . . the Parisians of Senegal! There aren't many of them but all the land round here belongs to them. They are craftier than the others. They always ask but never give anything away. Look, my brother-in-law is a bank manager and I married his sister; I feed her the whole time but he gives me nothing.

I won't let my daughter marry a Lébou because the Lébou always wants to dominate and I don't like that.

The Tukulor are good Muslims; they aren't too ambitious. They can be content with little. I'd let my daughter marry a Tukulor because Tukulor and Sarakolé practise their religion in the same way. I don't know the

Diola and I don't even want to know them because they aren't completely Muslim. I find them very difficult to understand.

I wouldn't let my daughter marry a Diola, because he wouldn't have the same character or the same religion as we do.

The Serer are hard-working and are good farmers. I would be quite prepared to take a Serer wife. Serer women manage well but the men don't look after their wives and that's why I wouldn't let my daughter marry a Serer.

The Nar are good Muslims but they think only of their own race. Well now, everyone is the same. We're all descended from Adam and Eve. I wouldn't let my daughter marry a Nar because he wouldn't even seek to get married to her.

The Lebanese here are businessmen and they're worse than all the other people in the collection of races you find in Senegal. The Lebanese regard the Africans as lower than the dogs they have at home.

I refuse to let my daughter marry a Lebanese.

The Cape Verde islanders are like the Lebanese. Here, you can marry a Portuguese girl, but a Portuguese man never marries a Wolof girl.

The metis are all right because they can change their religion and become Muslims, marrying African men and women.

The Toubab are all right. They are all right so far as they and their own interests are concerned. They don't make us work to no purpose. You can die for a Toubab but a Toubab will never die for an African. We went to war for them but they will never come and fight for us.

I would not let my daughter marry a Toubab because he wouldn't be of the same religion as my daughter.

Interview with Mr I

Mr I was 37 years old and belonged to the Khasanké[1] ethnic group. He had no religion. He was married to a Frenchwoman.

Mr I thought that the Malinké of Eastern Senegal, the Diola of Casamance and the Bassari had had their lot improved since independence, because they were neglected in the past.

He pointed out that, in order to defend their language, the Tukulor were unwilling to have a Wolof hegemony. He thought the Europeans were 'colonialists'. In his opinion, many of the businessmen and co-operation people were there to make money. They were not interested in the way the country was going. All that mattered to them was their own future.

1. Ethnic group belonging to the Mandingo family.

Bearing all that in mind, I don't have much liking for them.

In fifteen years' time we shall be back in the pre-colonial situation. I think that unemployment will play its part in this. At the present time, in Senegal, there are fifty Senegalese graduates out of work. There is anti-French feeling in the air and this is dangerous. In fact, it is not the French being here which annoys people but the inequality in situation. With equal qualifications, the French get a better deal than the Senegalese.

What I appreciate in them is their organizing ability, their rational approach and certain aesthetic tastes. I loathe their superiority complex and their colonialist spirit. Even left-wing people aren't any good. The people on the left should first of all improve the living conditions of the European workers before setting out to save the Third World. You find they haven't done anything in that direction.

You shouldn't expect too much from the Europeans and you must try to see things as they really are.

Interviews with Moors

It became apparent during our interviews with the Moors that they generally adapt themselves easily to the Senegalese environment but more particularly to the Wolof environment. The Muslim faith and the Wolof language are the essential factors making such integration possible.

It is to be noted that Moorish women have more contacts with the Senegalese than the men, because it is the women who go to the market and maintain neighbourly relations. Integration of the Moorish women is easier and more pronounced. A few Moorish girls marry Senegalese men in spite of their parents' refusal, these preferring their daughters to marry Moors.

It should also be noted that the Senegalese as a whole, while being hospitable, sometimes show a certain contempt for the Moors, who are aware of this.

Interview with Mr A

Mr A was a Moor aged 29. He had never been to a French school but was at that time attending evening classes (beginner's level).

Mr A had been in Dakar for a year. He did not associate with any Senegalese. He knew some but had never been interested in going to their homes. Nevertheless, Mr A told us that he would not like to associate with young Senegalese of his own age:

The young Senegalese go dancing but I could not go with them because of my religion. In fact, my religion forbids you to go dancing or to do as you please.

On the subject of marriage between Moors and Senegalese, Mr A told us:

I know that it isn't easy. My parents still follow the traditional ways very much, whereas here, people are more sophisticated than the Moors. There would also be conflict because my family wouldn't agree to my marrying a foreign girl. I can only marry a Moorish girl if I want to live in harmony with my family.

Mr A thought that the Senegalese were in general very hospitable.

I very much like the way the Senegalese behave towards foreigners. They aren't ill-natured. What I also appreciate in Senegal is that people are free to do what they want.

He nevertheless deplored the attitude of some Senegalese:

I find that the Moors are not very highly thought of because of their lack of cleanliness, and this is due to the fact that we don't have a very advanced way of life. The Senegalese criticize the Moors and insult them and I don't like that. The Moors have been living in Senegal for a long time and have long been in contact with the Senegalese and I think they ought to regard one another as brothers. The Senegalese can give the Moors advice but they ought not to run them down in front of everybody. That hurts me, but I can do nothing about it.

The Senegalese aren't lazy. I know some Wolofs who do any kind of job.

Mr A was not thinking of settling down in Senegal. He had come to Dakar to look for work and was employed as a messenger. He sent everything he earned back to his family.

I'm not very well off; all my family are dependent on me, my brothers, my sisters and my mother; my father died not long ago. I shall go back to Mauritania if my work doesn't enable me to stay here.

Interview with Mr B

Mr B was a Mauritanian aged 37. He had been to an Arab school and held the Arab elementary-school certificate. At the time, Mr B was a civil servant.

He had come to Senegal for the first time in 1939 and left again in 1951. He had been living in Dakar since 1959 and would go to Mauritania only to spend a few days. Mr B had relations in St Louis (father, mother, brothers and sisters). He was very well known in St Louis and in Dakar.

I don't have many Mauritanian friends and I have closer ties with the Senegalese. I have much more esteem for the Wolof but I have no contacts with the Diola and the Serer because I don't understand their languages.

Mr B told us that his wife was a Moorish woman but she was born in St Louis, spoke Moorish very badly and tended to have Senegalese ways. On the question of marriage between Mauritanians and Senegalese, Mr B said:

I don't see anything wrong in it because the main thing is that the husband and wife should be able to understand each other. My first wife was a Wolof. We loved each other but she just had some bad habits. With the Mauritanians, it is customary for the women to stay at home and not to go out with the men. We don't beat women. To begin with, I advised my wife to behave differently but it was no use. We were divorced after two years of marriage. My parents had not been shocked by my choice; they found it quite natural. I have many relations who have married Wolofs.

Mr B told us that he had travelled a lot and felt more at ease in Senegal than anywhere else.

Settling in Senegal or Mauritania is the same thing for me. I have all my property here. Previously, I had a shop, and all the money I had stayed in Senegal; I sent nothing to Mauritania. Now I have a better job. I don't know what the future has in store for me but I feel more comfortable here than in Mauritania.

Mr B did not belong to any association but when there were sacrifices to be made at the mosque he took part in them with the Senegalese and also when there were burials.

Mr B thought that it was easier for a Moor to live with the Wolof than with the others (Serer, Diola, etc.):

When a Mauritanian comes to Senegal he becomes a Wolof, and when a Wolof goes to Mauritania he becomes a Mauritanian, but a Mauritanian never becomes a Serer or a Diola. The Mauritanian is closer to the Wolof. But I could never live with the Diola or the Serer because we don't share the same religion or the same ways.

The Senegalese aren't lazy and they will take on any kind of job. Throughout Africa, Abidjan, Guinea, you find lots of Senegalese who are shoe-makers and tailors and who work very hard.

Interview with Miss C

Miss C was a Moorish girl aged 22. She was unmarried. She was born in Senegal (Dakar) and had only been to the Koranic school. Miss C told us:

I'm a Senegalese or at least I think of myself as one because I was born here and have Senegalese ways. Sometimes I wear traditional Moorish dress. Sometimes I put on a long African dress like the Senegalese women. I have many more contacts with the Wolofs. I've three friends who are Wolof; they've been well brought up and are serious-minded girls. They don't go out and they haven't had any children before getting married; pray God that it may be the same for me. The other Senegalese girls in the district however, do things I don't like, they go out at night and keep bad company.

I feel at home in Senegal and I've never felt any hostility of any kind. I know that when I am not there, the Senegalese girls and neighbours must criticize me; after all, I can't be liked by everybody.

On the subject of marriage between Mauritanians and Senegalese Miss C told us:

There are marriages which succeed and others which end up in divorce. I think that when a Senegalese man marries a girl from Mauritania it's because he loves her, with her customs, her way of dressing and her clothes. If the woman wants to please her husband, she can adopt the traditional Senegalese dress. There are some Senegalese who have no respect for the Mauritanians and when they've seen one they think they have known them all. Those are the kind of Senegalese who, when they've married a Mauritanian girl, make her unhappy, beat her, insult her and say to her: 'After all, you're nothing but a Mauritanian.' There's no Mauritanian who wants to marry me as yet and my parents would like me to marry a fellow-countryman. But if I see a Senegalese who loves me and whom I love, and if he has a good job, I would marry him without hesitation.

Miss C belonged to certain young people's associations. She went to the *sabar* (traditional Wolof dance) and when there were suppers, she went to them with her girl-friends.

Miss C thought that Senegalese women were dirty but that you couldn't really generalize:

There are some Senegalese women who are well brought up, their husbands don't earn very much but they manage to balance the budget and keep their house well. Sometimes however, the women are educated and go out to work but all they think of is clothes; they spend their time on themselves while their houses are dirty and badly kept.

Miss C said that, at the present time, everybody ought to work:

It's a duty for men to work. In Senegal, however, some men are educated (particularly the young ones) but instead of looking for work, they lounge about the district, smoking Indian hemp and making up to the women. At the present time, it's quite wrong to see people who don't work. I have had no education and I haven't got a job; that hurts me because I would have liked to have a trade.

Miss C preferred to stay in Senegal rather than to go and settle in Mauritania.

I'm much more attached to Senegal. I go to Mauritania from time to time and I have relations there; I'm pleased to see them but I shouldn't like to live there all the time.

Interview with Mr D

Mr D was a 69-year-old Moor. He came to Senegal when he was twelve and had not been back to Mauritania again until 1958 (when he went for a ten-day visit). He told us:

My parents died at Louga; my parents had all their possessions in Senegal. As for me, I'm a Senegalese Moor.

Mr. D is an important person:

I've been a jack-of-all-trades, I've been in business and was a butcher for a long time. I went into politics in 1946. At the moment, I'm a clerk of the court; I settle disputes between Moors and Tukulor.

In spite of the office he holds, Mr D is not liked by the Senegalese:

I have very superficial contacts with the Senegalese, particularly the Wolof. They aren't straight. I don't think the same way as they do. The Senegalese say that I'm not a Moor any more because I have a stone-built house and a telephone. They think the Moors are the lowest of the low. They don't want me to have responsibilities and would like them to go only to Senegalese like themselves. I've had a variety of jobs since 1949 and I've never been criticized and never been in debt. A Senegalese wouldn't have been able to shoulder his responsibilities properly. If he'd been in my place he would have done stupid things. The Wolof and the Lébou are proud and they can't stand foreigners. They say that the country belongs to them and that this is their home.

Mr D belongs to the Moorish association of Senegal.

I don't belong to any other association. I can't work with the Senegalese because they don't like me. I'm in close contact only with the government.

Mr D told us what he thought about marriage between Moors and Senegalese:

Marriage between Moors, Socé, Tukulor or Bambara is a good thing. But when a Moor marries a Wolof girl it's a disaster. The Wolof woman will stay with her husband as long as he has any money but when the husband hasn't got anything left she goes looking for a lover and abandons her husband. All the same, if my daughter wants to marry a Senegalese (particularly a Wolof) I wouldn't say no, but I would just lay down certain conditions: he mustn't make my daughter miserable (she must have food, clothes and especially I wouldn't like her to be beaten). If he didn't observe these conditions after the marriage, I would take my daughter back again.

Mr D told us that the Senegalese didn't like working:

It's the men with money who corrupt women, that's why Senegalese women don't want to go out to work. The Bambara, Tukulor and Moors work but not the Wolof. The Senegalese are parasites and live on other people when they are healthy and able to work. The Senegalese are not conscientious and when you give them an important job they do nothing, they are extravagant and think about nothing but having a good time.

Mr D told us that he would not go back to Mauritania again.

This is my home; I've got peace and quiet and I have all my property in Senegal.

Interview with Mr E

Mr E was a Mauritanian aged 44. He was a driver-mechanic. He had come to settle in Dakar in 1950. He knew many Senegalese:

I've known the Senegalese for a long time. I live with them, we work together and they regard me as a brother.

He told us:

I married a Moorish girl born in Senegal and my children were born in Senegal. It didn't matter to me whether I married a Mauritanian or a

Senegalese but it just happened that I loved a Mauritanian, so I married her. But if I were to take a second wife, I think she'll be a Wolof.

Mr E had been at Pikine since 1958:

I attend meetings when the district chief summons us. I pay my contribution when payments have to be made towards the building of a mosque.

When I left Mauritania, I chose Senegal because it was closer to home. I haven't had any trouble since I've been here; people have never said hurtful things to me and this is the place where I learnt my trade and began to work. The first time I went looking for a job it was the Senegalese who helped me.

Mr E did not consider going back to Mauritania.

I've built a house in Senegal, my children are at school here and they are more Senegalese than Moorish because they speak nothing but Wolof. I feel myself very close to the Senegalese. I can go and work in Mauritania but I feel more comfortable here. I don't stay long when I go to Mauritania because I'm immediately homesick for Dakar.

Interviews with metis

In the course of our interviews with metis, we found evidence, on the one hand of a feeling of superiority on their part and, on the other, of a sense of frustration on the part of African Senegalese, resulting in mutual discrimination and expressions of hostility between the Senegalese and the metis.

In their relations, there is often a gulf between the two, with the Africans on the one side and the metis on the other.

There are a few exceptions however. It appears that some metis have contacts with Senegalese who have the same affinities and habits as themselves. These African Senegalese are either Roman Catholics or Muslims of superior social status who have had a higher education.

Some African Senegalese maintain good relations with the metis. When speaking in abstract terms, however, distrust of and animosity towards what is not African appear. The metis believe that there is discrimination over names in admission to competitions and various examinations. Names which do not sound Senegalese are crossed out and replaced by truly Senegalese names and for this reason one finds metis taking their mother's name.

There are signs of a change taking place and for some people neither religion nor race is an obstacle.

The outlook of the metis appears to be changing and the following may be noted:
1.   Those who have changed somewhat in spite of themselves, or in other words who have been forced to have direct contacts with the African Senegalese since independence. These have re-

mained sectarian. They do not feel comfortable in Senegal and would prefer to go to Brazil, which they think of as the ideal country.

2. There are those who are really changing, who want to break down the metis outlook and who are doing something about it. These are in favour of race mixture.

Interview with Mrs A

Mrs A was a metis from St Louis and a Muslim by religion. Her father was a (genuine) native of St Louis and her mother a Viet-Namese. Mrs A married a metis from St Louis who also had a Viet-Namese mother. Mrs A was 31 years old and a teacher. She had been to the Secondary Teacher Training College and the Dakar Faculty of Arts (Propédeutique). She held the junior secondary teacher's certificate (CAP CEG).

Her Senegalese colleagues (teachers at the junior secondary school) are not very forthcoming: 'That may be due to the fact that I'm a woman and was just dropped into this division.' Sometimes, at meetings, 'they think of me as foreign and give me answers like this: "We Senegalese have a heritage to preserve . . . ." '

I have a Senegalese name, there's no doubt about that. It hurts me, though, to see how I'm treated; I mean they make me feel I have a Senegalese name but I'm not Senegalese. You see, when I have an appointment at the ministry, for example, or with the inspector, they greet me with astonishment saying 'Oh! You're Mrs X . . .'.

She found all these things offensive and said that, to get on in Senegal, you had to be either black or white but not of mixed blood because the metis were victimized.

She did not have any really close Senegalese friends. She was on friendly terms with some Senegalese but had found, from experience, that, in conversation, people were always saying things like 'Oh, you metis . . . '.

They regard us as people apart and that's why we associate with other metis. Some people think that the metis are stuck up but that's because they're rejected by the Africans.

It's all just a question of the colour of your skin because there are Senegalese whose names are not at all Senegalese (Dumont, King, etc.) but they're accepted just the same because their skins are black.

No, I don't belong to the UPS and I don't take any interest in politics. All the same, I don't approve of the government's education policy. I think the government is weak. [This was in reference to the Commission on the Life of Secondary and Technical Schools.] The representatives of the pupils at junior secondary and grammar schools are demanding several things including participation in the teachers' council and in drawing up the rules, and abolition of examinations, and the government appears to be willing to accept everything. I think you need authority and discipline in bringing up adolescents. I think the government ought to deal with more urgent problems like the adaptation of education to life in the country as it is.

The Senegalese are idle and indolent. They object to doing certain jobs, so that they are driven to begging. For a foreigner, this is a sign of laziness. And they're not conscientious about their work: a teacher stays at home without telling the school, just to wait for somebody who is going to visit her. And when I think that I leave my child ill at home and go to work! I tell them and then I pop back home to see the child. You need a minimum of conscientiousness when all's said and done. The Senegalese, and they're the majority, won't stick at things. One of the teachers in the school where I am thought that twenty-one hours of lessons a week was too much. He preferred to be a supply teacher, so that he can come when he wants. The children, incidentally, have seen how things are and are asking for efficient, conscientious teachers.

In general the Senegalese are hospitable, but they're conceited, too, and often envious. They are tending to adopt bourgeois ways, they like luxury and aren't responsible enough; they live from hand to mouth. They're capable of spending all the money they have in the world without bothering about tomorrow. The women say this sort of thing: 'What's the good of saving, who for? If we make our husband rich, he'll marry another wife.' They don't think of leaving anything to their children; the only heritage is that a child should have a job later on.

The Senegalese think that Senegal will be 'Dakarized' in a few years' time. Dakar will become modern and the rest of the country will remain poor. Senegal won't change in a few years. The students who have inherited a mixture of colonialism and traditional society are floundering about. I don't know if modern ideas will win the day. The young people in the village are attached to the traditional society and the nucleus of intellectuals will not be able to rule everything. There's a revolution going on among the women, all the same. They are claiming respect and are refusing to be treated as men's slaves. In a few years, the women will be more like the European women and it's the women who will show that there has been a change. The men won't change.

I think that Muslim marriage should be made a serious business. There's no contract as there is in a Christian marriage and the marriage may take place with the man in St Louis and the woman in Dakar. People ought to have to come before the mayor and that would perhaps alter the way men behave.

On the subject of technical assistance, Mrs A told us:

We still need them. The only thing is, are they playing their part? I think that in fact they're not trying to train the Senegalese. They're doing all they can to stay here as long as possible and to make people believe they're indispensable. It's not a matter of not having enough patience, it's intentional, they don't want to train the Senegalese.

Mrs A came to St Louis when she was 9 years old. She grew up in St Louis but had paid short visits to France (two months, one month and a half), while on holiday. She would like to travel and live in a different country.

There are times when I feel homesick for my native country, Viet-Nam. I should like to go to Madagascar or Brazil. Since there are a lot of metis in those countries, I think that I should have been better understood and I think that I'd feel myself much more at home in those countries than here [in Senegal].

Having been brought up by her mother in Viet-Nam, she was very unfavourably affected by the first contact she had with her father's family. The first words which her paternal grandparents said to her father were,

'Why did you marry a foreign girl when there are women here?' I remember saying to my mother: 'We'll make an application to France so that we can go back home.' Our relations with my father's family are superficial. My brother gets on better because, when he was small, he used to go and play with his friends. They used to call him 'Chinese' but he got used to that. He was even going to marry a Senegalese [a real one], but he lost heart and said that it wasn't the right thing. Then our relations on our father's side kept saying: 'Aren't there enough beautiful Senegalese girls for you to marry?'

Mrs A's father had died three years previously. There was now practically no contact with her father's relations.

We say hello to them occasionally but we don't go out of our way to do so. . . .

Mrs A told us that racialism exists. She told us about the misfortunes of her sister-in-law who married a (real) Senegalese.

The parents of my sister-in-law's husband are forcing him to take a [real] Senegalese as a second wife. Like that, they say, we'll have grandchildren who are really ours. My sister-in-law has got four children by her husband but his parents have rejected them. . . .

Interview with Mr B

Mr B was aged 30 and was a Muslim metis from St Louis. He had a law degree and held a diploma of the ENAS.[1] Mr B worked as a civil servant.

He was on very good terms with his office colleagues and thought that he had been accepted by them. Talking about his friends, Mr B told us:

I've only got Senegalese friends. Most of them are Wolof and they're childhood friends I had in St Louis. I've never been conscious of any discrimination and that's perhaps due to the fact that I'm a Muslim because religion matters a lot in Senegal.

There were however, some small things to which he had, in any case, grown accustomed—which showed him that certain Senegalese did not regard him entirely as one of themselves.

For example, two days ago I was invited to a Muslim baptism. They offered us some *lakh*.[2] They presented a bowl to all my friends with water for them to wash their hands but I was the only one to whom they gave a spoon. They may have been treating me as a Catholic perhaps but I don't think so, for if the Catholic had been a black-skinned Senegalese they would have offered him the bowl. Because I'm a metis, they thought straight away that I would behave like a Westerner, in other words, someone who eats at table, etc. I think it's also due to the fact that I never wear a boubou.

Mr B did not belong to any association. He went to trade-union meetings rather unwillingly. He said this was due to shyness:

I'm terrified by nature of having certain responsibilities within an association.

1. École Nationale d'Administration du Sénégal.
2. Millet porridge with curds, usually served in a big calabash.

In Mr B's view, the Senegalese could not be said not be conscientious but they lost interest in their work through discouragement.

The Senegalese are no lazier than anyone else. The only thing is we sometimes get discouraged and are impatient to have everything straight away. As we can't have everything we want all at once, we lose our enthusiasm.

On the subject of technical assistance, Mr B stated:

For the time being, we can't do without them in certain sectors where we have not enough higher grade personnel. But it's both a good and a bad thing. Technical assistance ought to provide training in good faith and make way when everything's going smoothly. The only thing is they shouldn't rush off when they go. It's better for them to remain as long as we need them.

On the other hand, Mr B said:

The Senegalese aren't inefficient and they can run the departments they are in charge of. Everything depends on their training. Most of the élite in Senegal have been trained in French universities and there's no reason why they should be less able than the French. They're up to the job, provided they're put in a similar situation.

On the topic of certain characteristics of the Senegalese, Mr B admitted:

We Senegalese sometimes compromise the ends because we take no account of the means available. We thus make promises which we can't keep.

Mr B was not married; speaking of the choice of his future wife, he said:

I shall marry a Senegalese girl belonging to any ethnic group provided she's the modern, educated sort. Love knows no frontiers.

Relations with his father's family were not very good. Mr B's mother was a Viet-Namese and his father was from St Louis.

Since my father died, my relations on my father's side are a bit touchy about some of the things I do, and they put a twist on everything. They think that because the link between us [my father] is not there any more I'm abandoning them. In fact it's nothing of the kind but it's obvious that I can't do for them what my father used to do when he was alive.

If Mr B had the chance of going to live elsewhere he would go to France:

I'd like to go back to France because it's a country I know and I went to university there. All the same, I shouldn't like to go for good because there are too many things binding me to Senegal.

Mr B thought that Senegalese women would change, particularly in the big towns. They would be like Western women in ten years' time.

Interview with Mr D

Mr D was a metis from St Louis, and a Roman Catholic by religion. He was 44 years old and married to a Senegalese metis.

Mr D had six years' secondary education and worked in a bank.

He was on friendly terms with his colleagues. He got on well with everybody. He had not been conscious of any hostility towards himself and said:

I've a few Senegalese friends but no intimate friends. My real friends are Europeans or metis. They're friends I've had since I was a child. I haven't any real Senegalese friends and this is due to my upbringing. I was brought up in St Louis and the metis belong to the upper class; they had a French culture. It was unthinkable for a metis to be seen with a Senegalese and the Senegalese were kept on one side. Since independence, the Senegalese are tending to take their revenge. They remember the humiliations they suffered in the past and they blame us.

On the question of marriage between metis and Senegalese, Mr D told us:

When the man and woman are both Catholics, there's no problem because their way of life is the same; they have the same education, the same affinities, they eat at table, etc. But when the woman is a Catholic metis and her husband is a Muslim Senegalese, it just won't work because their way of life isn't the same, unless the man's sophisticated and not too much a stickler for his religion. Otherwise, the husband takes a second or a third wife and the wife who is a metis suffers and this leads to divorce. I think that, in marriage, religion is of more importance than the colour of one's skin or one's ethnic group.

Mr D used to belong to certain associations in St Louis (sports and cultural associations) but he had now dropped everything because he did not have enough time.

Mr D thought that the Senegalese were no lazier than anyone else; as in all countries, there were hard workers and idlers. On the subject of technical assistance, Mr D told us:

We must have them in certain branches but we could do without them in others. The technical-assistance people come here to save as much as possible and send all their money back to France. They don't make trade flourish and they don't contribute to economic development. Twenty years ago, the French were worth while and worked a lot. Now they know that they're here only for a year or two and they don't do any real work and don't train you well. In some sectors, we have good top-grade staff and we can look after things for ourselves. Our bank runs without any technical assistants. A few years ago, the situation was catastrophic. The technical-assistance people who had been dismissed said that the bank would not keep going for more than a year, but it's been running for four years now. Things were put right by the Senegalese on their own.

Mr D thought that there were differences between the various categories of Senegalese. The Wolof were proud and lazy; the Serer were pleasant, hard-working and responsible. He preferred the people from Casamance because they were responsible and hard-working and he got on better with them because they were not so proud as the Wolof.

Mr D told us:

The women of Senegal are changing. Previously they didn't know how to look after a house and were illiterate but now they're becoming intellectuals. The men, for their part, are refusing to marry a girl chosen by their parents and prefer to marry a girl of their own choice who has more or less the same intellectual level as themselves and who is modern and educated.

Mr D would like to live in France but not to work there.

Interview with Mr E

Mr E was a metis from St Louis, aged 29 and a Roman Catholic by religion. He had an arts degree and was a bank clerk.

On the question of his relations with his colleagues in the bank, Mr E said:

We're on good terms and I've never had any trouble with them. They look on me as a Senegalese. When there are problems specific to Senegal they come and ask me. I'm regarded as fully Senegalese and when there are training courses my name is put forward for them.

Mr E had only Senegalese friends.

I haven't any French friends although my father is a Frenchman and my mother a metis. I fit into the African background more easily than into the European.

Mr E said that there was discrimination by name:

When they find a name which doesn't sound Senegalese—Boucher for example—on the list of successful candidates in an examination of Senegalese for a training course, they simply cross it out and put a N'Diaye or Diouf in its place. The metis is thus handicapped from the start because his name gets him put on one side. I can say that, in the abstract, there is a certain racialism and a distrust of everything which isn't Senegalese. You will find metis nowadays taking their mothers' names: N'Diaye, Diop, etc., so that they have more chance of getting through an examination or of being sent abroad for training courses.

Mr E had married a Senegalese metis:

There was never any question of marrying a Senegalese, so far as I was concerned. Of course I had Senegalese girl friends but I'm sectarian in the matter of marriage. I think you have to put the sheep with the sheep and the goats with the goats. I feel uncomfortable when I see a mixed couple. I would never have married a Senegalese because we don't have the same upbringing. It's true that Senegalese women are becoming more and more sophisticated, more modern and Westernized but they still lack something. I can see a metis woman marrying a Senegalese, because it's the wife who looks after the house and does the entertaining. But I can't see a metis marrying a Senegalese girl. You can say what you like, but Senegalese women are dirty. When you go to their houses, the sitting room is clean and well kept but you mustn't look any further.

Mr E is a member of certain associations (sports and cultural) in the bank.

The young people feel that they have things to learn in the way of manners and they have a kind of complex. I think that the Senegalese tend to want me when it's a question of setting up a club or a centre because the metis are good at organizing things and are energetic and responsible. I'm not too keen on belonging to these associations because the Senegalese talk a lot but don't do anything.

The Senegalese isn't lazy; he's able enough but he doesn't take enough pains. In the bank, they make plans but never get to the final stage. The Senegalese is a dreamer, unstable and frivolous. On the other hand, there are some who are too serious and who are sometimes pedantic.

We still need technical assistance in some fields like medicine and technology but there are some people who shouldn't be here; that creates misunderstandings and conflicts.

The Senegalese is obliging; all you need is to have his confidence. He makes friends very quickly. I've got friends practically everywhere and I can manage all right when anything goes wrong. That may be a bad thing because, in Senegal, if you don't know anybody, you can't manage to get what you want through the ordinary channels.

Mr E told us that he would like to live in Brazil:

I'd like to live in Brazil because, away over there, you have problems only if you aren't a metis. I feel at home in Senegal but not completely at ease. Of course I speak the language, which is an advantage. I think the ones who harm the metis are the metis who think of themselves as Europeans, feel superior to the Senegalese and make it obvious.

Interviews with Lebanese

It became clear in our interviews with the Lebanese that many of them, and incidentally, those who are most racialist in outlook, seek to identify themselves with the French. The reference point is French education. 'Outside, I'm just like them.'

All the same, the Lebanese are not always keen on the French because at the moment most Lebanese are in business and their firms are in competition with French firms. It should be noted that the Lebanese often have Senegalese nationality, which exempts them from payment of certain taxes imposed on foreign businesses. Competition between the Lebanese and the French is liable to become still keener because the young Lebanese are studying subjects which will make it possible for them to take over the senior jobs when the French technical assistants leave.

Differences between East and West are also of great importance for the Lebanese, particularly with regard to marriage. Lebanese men criticize French women for not being able to adapt to Lebanese ways, which involve welcoming anybody at any time.

Criticisms of the Wolof became apparent mainly when comparisons were made with other ethnic groups. The majority of the people we interviewed stated that the Africans were incapable of running a business both because they lacked ability, owing to the ethnic group to which they belonged, and also because they did not have the right qualifications. There were very few Lebanese who would tolerate marriage between an African woman and a Lebanese man or between an African man and a Lebanese woman. Some of them even felt an almost physical revulsion for the blacks.

Relations between the Lebanese and the Africans, even though mainly in business matters, were nevertheless on a larger scale than existed between the French and the Africans. The Lebanese ended up by feeling more or less at home in Senegal. Many of them told us that they felt more at ease in Dakar than in the Lebanon. For a number of them, the fact of having been born in Senegal was important and they felt then that they more or less belonged to the country.

All the Lebanese thought that higher-grade personnel should be African but there were very few who were in favour of the Africanization of the higher personnel of their own particular sector especially the commercial sector. To justify this view, they spoke of the 'African's lack of organizational ability' or the 'lack of intellectual ability' and, finally, the 'lack of capital'.

Interview with Mr A
Mr A was 28 years old, a chemist, unmarried and a Roman Catholic

It's ridiculous to ask me who I'll marry. I'll marry the girl I love and it' a matter of taste and affinity. Not a black girl because that would give rise to too many problems, which are insoluble for the time being. Perhaps later on it will be easier. I'm not against it but it's difficult, unthinkable I'll marry any white girl but not a black or a yellow or a red-skinned girl In any case, I can't see myself falling in love with one, at least I haven' done so yet. The colour doesn't bother me too much but it's the present state of our habits and customs which makes marriage with a person of another colour impossible. There are too many complications and I just won't do it. It's more for social reasons than because of racialist prejudices It's the same for religion. It's just as important as race. I'm not against people of different religions getting married and I may perhaps fall in love with a Muslim but we haven't yet reached a sufficient degree of maturity for this to be possible. For example, if I married a Lebanese Muslim, there would be problems with both the families, and if the girl was of a different colour and a Muslim too, that would be catastrophic

I have nothing to do with the Wolof.

The Tukulor are shoe-shine boys and *borom table*.[1]

The Serer are fighters.

The Lébou are the richest landowners on the Cape Verde peninsula

I know the Moors very well, they are very troublesome customer

---

1. Literally, the man at the table, a man who sells various objects spread out on a stall.

They smell very nasty and are excellent walkers: when you run after them, you can't catch them up.

French girls are very charming, gracious and elegant. Frenchmen are very witty. They are pleasant to get on with.

About the Lebanese, I can't tell you. Is this really anonymous? I like my Lebanese fellow-countrymen because they have a sense of honour and hospitality, honour at all levels, money, women. That you can't deny them. But I criticize them for treating a person as important only if he has money. Even if a person is illiterate, he might become a real leader. And I have actual cases in mind, I'm not just speaking theoretically. A lot of them are unscrupulous and the main thing as far as they are concerned is to make money. They go to prison but they make money and so they're respected in spite of everything. If I might say what I feel about Lebanon itself, I think that justice was never so easily bought as there.

What I think about my daughter's marrying into any of these ethnic groups is this: I'm a good, solid Lebanese and, theoretically, she'll marry the sort of person I marry myself. But in twenty years, things will perhaps have changed. It might even be better to marry a black than a white. It's just the social problems and the difficulties.

African art? Well, really, I'm not an artist, I'm a chemist. I don't like it and know only what the *bana-bana* [illicit street venders] sell. I like the masks worked in gold for cuff-links. But, to tell the truth, I know nothing about it. It's like Picasso's paintings: I don't understand them at all and I don't like them. Sometimes the masks are very attractive but generally they aren't very delicately carved. And in any case the people selling them often try to make you believe that they've got genuine stuff and they try to sell you Sudan mahogany for ebony.

I know nothing at all about African literature. But, you know, I work and I'm busy and I don't have much time. I know nothing about it, except Senghor. I don't understand his poems very well. All that sort of thing is very pretty but really, it's perhaps too deep for me. As I told you, I'm only a chemist; I'm not a literary man.

I employ three Africans and a metis woman for selling in my shop and handling goods. It's natural to employ natives, we're in their country. Africanization in my sector is a regular thing and they're quite capable of doing the work. There are some who are better at it than I am and I'm in favour. You have to follow the trend. It may be premature but this is the way you've got to go. This is the way things are going. Africanization can be carried out in other sectors too, maybe too early, maybe too late, but in itself it's only to be expected. You can't hope for the same output as when the Europeans were here but that's because they need time to get accustomed to the job. But the thing in itself is quite natural and I'm in favour of it. There's an Arabic proverb which says: 'The wise man takes life as it comes.'

There is not enough co-operation and it doesn't go far enough, but it is essential, especially inside the country. It must be continued until they wake up and become self-sufficient or else they will lose the benefit of what they have received from outside. Co-operation is necessary and must be increased until the Senegalese take over, which means several decades from now.

Interview with Mr B

Mr B was 35 years old and in business. He was married to a Lebanese whom he had known from childhood. He had two children and was a Roman Catholic, as was his wife. She did not work but stayed at home.

I married my wife because I had known her for a long time. To marry a woman of another race, well that depends. Yes, why not; I'd marry a non-Lebanese white all right, if I loved her. But not a black or a woman of another colour, not a yellow-skinned woman. I can't say why. I don't know why. The idea has never entered my mind; I've never thought of it. I just got married for love.

There are lots of mixed couples but, to take an example, a Lebanese woman married an African but left him and went back to the Lebanon.

With a woman of another religion, a Muslim for example, it doesn't matter at all. It's just the same and love is the only thing which counts.

I speak Wolof and I'm on visiting terms with Wolofs who are friends of mine. In any case, my father used to entertain everybody without bothering which race they belonged to. There are idlers and workers among the Wolof. All those I know are very hospitable. I was born in Senegal among the Africans and so far I haven't wanted to leave. Anyone who is born in a country can't just go off somewhere else. Like those who are in France—they can't come to Senegal. I went to settle in the Lebanon but I found it wasn't possible and I came back.

I've always had quite a bit to do with French people. I've a lot of friends whom I got to know in the clubs and I play bowls with them. Now I see them only at the clubs.

Yes, I know the Lebanese (but not the Syrians); it doesn't seem natural to say that I associate with them. I go to their houses and they come to mine; they're the ones I know most; we spend long evenings together when we're friends. My daughter will marry anyone she likes provided he's a responsible man and a decent sort. It depends on who he s and what sort of job he has because that's what matters to all parents. I don't bother about race. But I wouldn't be too happy if she married an African, I prefer someone of the same colour. Why? To answer you, I just have to say that it's never been done in our family. My parents don't agree. It's difficult to give you an answer. I don't know why exactly, it's just like that. If my daughter wants to marry someone of another religion, that's her business.

African art means nothing to me, I don't know anything about it. To be honest with you, no art interests me; I don't know anything about it at all. It's just the same with literature.

All my staff are Africans: they are salesmen and workers. My brother has a clothing factory and all his workers are Africans, too. In Senegal, you can't employ anyone else but Africans. I should prefer other people but you just can't.

I don't know whether Africanization of the senior staff in other sectors is a good thing. For commerce, it isn't good. They are idle, and gobble up all the money and aren't successful. You've heard about cases of misappropriation of money. If an African opens a business, he shuts down a month later because he's spent everything.

Co-operation is a good thing, yes. The Africans aren't very able and they don't have the intelligence of a white man or another race.

Interview with Mr C

Mr C was 50 and was a Lebanese Muslim businessman. His wife was of the same ethnic group and religion as himself. He had five children: two boys and three girls.

I might have married someone other than a Lebanese, a French girl or a Senegalese; in fact they're all the same. It's the same for religion. If I find a second girl, it doesn't matter who she is, provided I love her, I shall marry her.

The Wolof aren't bad. I've lived among them for thirty years and some of them are my friends. I don't know anything about the others.

The Moors, they're all right.

The French, they're like the rest.

The Syrio-Lebanese as well, a lot of them are friends of mine because we're from the same country. I'd let my daughter marry anyone, even a Chinese, even a Japanese if she likes, why not?

I don't know anything about African art and African literature.

I've got six Africans with me as driver-delivery men and watchmen. They've been with me a long time and I've kept them on.

Africanization of higher personnel in other sectors isn't natural, everyone has got to earn his living. I'm not a bit in favour of Africanization in commerce, it's bad for the country and discourages people.

Co-operation is good for giving advice to the country but it should come to an end as soon as people can manage for themselves.

Interview with Mr E

Mr E was 24 years old. He was a Roman Catholic, a student and unmarried.

If I were to get married, and if I had to choose between a Lebanese girl and a Senegalese, I'd choose the first. Personally, I'm not concerned about race but society makes you think of it. You can't help thinking, in particular, about what people will say. There aren't the same problems with a European woman, but with an Asian, other than an Arab of course, it would be just the same as marrying an African woman. Religion doesn't enter into it at all, it doesn't affect me; it's something quite separate. If I marry a woman, it will be for what she is herself, for the understanding between us, for reasons of sentiment. The main thing is that I should like her, without bothering about her social status or her religion.

The Wolof are likeable people, friendly-disposed but too sentimental. You can do anything, absolutely anything, with them if you play on their sentiments. They are very egoistic but very sociable, which makes it possible for us to be on very friendly terms.

The Serer are very religious, kindlier than the Wolof, and very obliging. I think that, unlike the Wolof, who have a certain superiority complex, they consider themselves inferior to the whites.

The Tukulor remind me of Arab slaves, in the sense that when they're attached to you, you can get them to do anything. They are racialist, not only as regards the whites but as regards all other races. They live closed in on themselves and get excited for nothing at all.

The Sarakolé are thought of as foreigners and not as Senegalese because of their accent, for example. They're real robots. If you need a bodyguard, employ a Sarakolé. For him, an order is an order; that's the difference in comparison with the Wolof, who are much more accommodating.

The Diola think of themselves as belonging to Casamance and not as Senegalese. They speak of 'Casamance', not Senegal, as their country. They're rather like the Bretons in France. They're very pleasant and very obliging. Most of them are Catholics and religion (as in the case of the Serer) has a lot to do with making them what they are. The Catholic will always refer back to God, will be a fervent believer and very humanistic. The Muslim will believe in his marabout more than in God, he'll spend everything on himself and I think he is, shall we say, more fatalistic.

The Cape Verde islanders are a great mixture of races. They are a group apart and don't form part of the society.

The Moors are a group on their own as well. They know that they are here as foreigners who have come to do business. They have friends only among themselves and don't like the blacks at all.

There are two kinds of French people. First, those who have always lived here or at least have lived here a long time. These are the colonial French who regard the Africans more or less as slaves. They are very racialist. Second, those who have just arrived and who are here for a year or two. To begin with they have some ideas of equality and treat the Africans as equals. They are more humane and more easily approachable but they close up very quickly because they go around the others, who very soon show them another kind of behaviour. You must have 'done' France to see this problem. The ones who live in France have a fairly low social status and live in complete equality. When they come to Senegal, they accept this equality to begin with but it takes only three or four months for them to have a feeling of superiority which arises from the fact that they are better dressed and eat better than the Africans in general.

There are two sorts of Lebanese as well. First, the rich; they've lived quite a long time here and exploit the black and use him to get rich. So long as they're paying, the black has to do as they say and they don't recognize that he has any rights. Second, the poor: they are much more directly in contact with the Africans and they share their problems and family difficulties. They take part in them. You find them in the most remote corners of Senegal; sometimes they could afford to get out of the up-country places but they have ties there and think of that as their true homeland. In any case, almost all the Lebanese who've been in Senegal for twenty years feel themselves at home here and only go to the Lebanon for holidays. They can't adapt themselves elsewhere to other living conditions and to another climate. The Lebanese give the impression that they're here for their business and that they don't help each other ('Every man for himself'). They do each other favours sometimes but they're all trying to get the better of their compatriots in business and seize every opportunity of doing so. On the other hand, you get a feeling that for the last couple of years the Lebanese have been unsure of themselves and, to take one example, are conscious of the need to join together. Friendly societies are being formed and clubs as well. It's a matter of security following government measures which are unfavourable to them. There really is this need to unite among them now.

The Syrians are different from the Lebanese and the Africans are closer to the Lebanese. The Syrians are very shut in on themselves and they deal only in textiles, which is special to them, whereas the Lebanese do a bit of everything, in 'bazaar'. The Syrians lack confidence and don't lend money, unlike the Lebanese who will take IOUs and give credit and who always find a way of getting their money back.

Personally, when I get married, it will be me and not my parents who will be involved. It's for me to choose to set up house and to take on responsibilities. It will be just the same for my daughter. I shall just give her advice and I'll let her marry anyone she thinks she can be happy with, even a black. But I'll make just one condition: that they won't live in Africa, because a black married to a white girl will have difficulties there, whereas in Europe they could be very happy. In Africa, the African goes back to his family, etc., and that gives rise to problems.

African art has remained in the pure, wild state. It's a pity that people tend to exploit it too much, which makes it lose its value. Take those marvellous statues of olden times, for example, which are reproduced and faked. The Senegalese had no idea of their value. It has been only in these last few years that they have discovered it. But now they are losing their original value because they're being made more and more for tourists.

African literature is too abstract and written by people who are too surrealistic. I don't like it, I'm too down-to-earth. Senegalese writers are trying to make a separate literature apart from French literature, although they've always lived with French literature and been steeped in it. Now they're trying to break away from its influence. But if they think in Wolof and translate their thoughts into French, it's ridiculous; although in Wolof their ideas mean something. It seems to me that, in this way, there is a false African literature.

African employees in general are exploited, even in the government. I am thinking of the civil servants. Where I work, there are four Africans employed as salesmen. They work 'like blacks', that's the only thing you can say, but they don't get on because they've got all their family on their hands and they're very handicapped from the medical point of view. They are in general much more conscious of being employees than the whites are, in the sense that, for the white man, twelve o'clock is knocking-off time, but not for them, they wait until their work is finished. I'm not using 'employee' in a derogatory sense, quite the reverse.

I'm for Africanization in sectors other than my own. If they are able people, obviously I'm in favour of it but generally they aren't. I'm prepared to accept it, but you must demand the right standards, so that you don't get someone with just the primary-school certificate in a senior post.

I'm in favour of the Africanization of my sector and that's very important. An African is more willing to confide in an African than in a white man. For example, all the Tukulor go to a Tukulor and you might have three unoccupied cashiers and one Tukulor cashier with a long queue in front of him. They would queue up to wait for the Tukulor but they wouldn't come to us. It's just the same for the white man. And it's only reasonable, here, to Africanize.

Co-operation is necessary for the time being because it makes it possible to develop tourism in Senegal. But it doesn't bring any profit to Senegal. Those employed in co-operation are housed and paid by France; they spend nothing and try to take as much money home with them as possible. It's those people above all who are creating that class of 'aristocrats'. They're some use, however, because there aren't enough competent people here. I think that co-operation will come to an end in, say, ten years' time.

Should a black man marry a white woman? While they're on their own it's all right. In France, it's quite all right but when they come back to Senegal, they both make problems for each other. When the white woman sees another white woman living in a different way from the way she does (queening it over her), she will feel she has gone down in the world. The black man will also want to go back to certain habits and certain customs. His wife keeps her customs and he will feel put out and they both go their own way.

A white man and a black woman? That is more likely to be a success. If he's a Lebanese, he fits into his wife's background, adapts to it and becomes black without having a black skin.

Interview with Mr F

Mr F was 45 years old; he was a Muslim Lebanese and in business.

I married a Lebanese girl, which is quite normal. I wouldn't have married any other because we wouldn't have had the same outlook. Particularly when you think of the children, you have to consider a bit. That doesn't stop marriage being a success between a Lebanese man and a European woman. With an African woman, it wasn't possible before the war, and an African woman wouldn't have suited a Lebanese for many reasons, such as habits and family life; even now I think a marriage like that can't succeed in most cases.

My wife is a Muslim like me but I might have married someone of another religion because that counts less than one's race.

I don't make any distinction between the Wolof and the others, and I speak of the Senegalese in general. I only know that my *fatou* [maids] are Serer and that they work very well, like the Diola. The Senegalese are likeable in general and I prefer them to the people from the Ivory Coast, whom I have known a bit. But I'm not on friendly terms with many Senegalese; most of my contacts with them are for business purposes.

I only have business relations with the Moors as well, that's all.

The Portuguese have a good name for painting and things like that.

Some of the Syrio-Lebanese, like the French, are all right. They're good workers but that doesn't stop them wanting to take advantage of competition. I have bonds of friendship and kinship with them. I associate most with them because we have the same outlook, the same ways and the same tastes.

My daughter will marry a Lebanese simply because of having the same ways of going on, and a Muslim because a small misunderstanding is enough to make religion become very important. And I would even prefer her to marry an Arab Muslim than a Catholic Lebanese.

African art isn't bad. I've seen a few pieces done by beginners. But statues and all that, they don't mean anything to me.

I haven't read any African literature.

I had some African staff once but not now because I work with my brother. It's natural to employ some when you need them and it's good, in fact better, for business because most of the customers are Africans.

Africanization of the higher personnel in all sectors is inevitable, so you have to be in favour of it.

It's the same for the commercial sector. But you mustn't do it too quickly. It must be done quite gradually for the African to be capable of taking on the responsibility for a store or shop or an administrative appointment. You have to accept it but it's a bit early.

Co-operation is very necessary in certain fields such as teaching and medicine. Co-operation in life is a normal sort of thing and there are no frontiers existing now.

Where mixed marriages between blacks and whites are concerned, I'll take the example of Lebanese I know who have married black women. There are good marriages which are a success and others which are failures. Sometimes the girl hasn't been educated for responsibility, particularly if she's just a girl the man has met. It's lucky, then, if the marriage succeeds. Marriage between members of one and the same ethnic group involves fewer risks.

Interview with Mrs G

Mrs G was 38, a Muslim Lebanese. She was a shopkeeper, married with six children. She had married a Muslim Lebanese.

I married someone I loved and that's all, that's the only reason. There was mutual understanding between us and I didn't pay any attention to his nationality or his religion. I couldn't have married an African, for questions of principle which I consider important, on which I take a very firm stand; I can't help it. In spite of the changes taking place, there are principles which you just can't sweep away like that because we've changed. Religion? I couldn't care less about it, I don't pay any attention to it.

I don't make any differentiation between the Senegalese. They're very nice and they are charming folk, whom you have to understand. They're a bit lazy and you have to show them how to work; they haven't much initiative but they are easy to direct and once you've put them on the right path they carry on by themselves.

Among the French, the old colonialists are very different from those who have recently come from France. Here, they think they're superior to people and are difficult to get on with.

The Lebanese are born businessmen. There's a certain amount of animosity among them but that doesn't mean that they don't help each other. They're very nice people although they've lots of faults, but it's not for me to say so.

My daughter can marry whom she likes. If she married a Senegalese, that would cause a lot of problems; I shall give her advice, and if she won't listen to me she can marry whom she likes.

I don't know anything at all about African art. I don't have anything to do with that sort of thing. My work takes up all my time.

I don't know anything at all about African literature. So I'm just not up in it.

I employ African salesmen. Speaking as a shopkeeper, it's very necessary to do so because the Africans are really only comfortable with an African salesman. They feel a bit awkward and shame-faced with me and they may buy simply because they don't dare refuse me. Whereas with another African, they say truthfully whether they like something or not.

It's too early for the Africanization of other sectors because there aren't enough competent people available. Africanization is possible but with European advisers. It's going to come sooner or later but when the young people are better educated, then it will be feasible.

In the commercial sector, we are about half-way with Africanization. It's better to let everybody bring in capital, as in the Ivory Coast, which is very prosperous. They're always in deficit here, customs duties are too high and that isn't a good thing for the country. Look at the Ivory Coast, they're rich.

Co-operation is a failure and those working on it do nothing at all. They just make money for themselves, that's all. Technical assistance?

Some assistance! They do nothing at all for the country. They don't spend any money and, if they didn't have to eat, they wouldn't buy anything at all.

I'm not in favour of mixed marriages because later on each party gets more and more complexes. I don't agree at all that 'the future lies with the metis'. Everybody ought to stay in their own circle because if they don't, there will always be complexes. You can't help it. Sooner or later the African goes back to his ways and, if he doesn't, he is rejected and that has an effect on him. I'm in favour of change. We are in the moon age but. . . .

Interviews with French people

These interviews were with Europeans living in Senegal. We asked them why they had come to Africa and to Senegal in particular. We then asked what they thought about Senegal, its future and the Senegalese. We talked with our informants about African literature, films and art.

We also tried to find out what relations there were between these Europeans and the various ethnic groups. It appeared that these were very limited, not to say non-existent.

Interview with Mr A

Mr A was a teacher, 47 years old. He had been in Senegal for fourteen years, having elected to go there through a desire for social service. He had taught for ten years in France without any sense of achievement. He had therefore decided, with his wife, to leave France and had chosen Senegal because he thought the Senegalese were better and more generous people (Senegalese infantry had been billeted in his wife's school at the end of 1944; his wife was pregnant at the time and the Senegalese gave them milk and bread and fed the baby).

He made it clear that neither he nor his wife had come to make money nor had they come because life in Senegal was easier than elsewhere. In any case, he practised a sort of redistribution of his goods: if he and his wife earned a great deal of money, they spent it locally (staff, etc.). He was doing a kind of lay missionary work trying to give a new meaning to his life.

He had arrived full of optimism, confidence and hope. He said, however, that he was rather disappointed by present-day Senegal because he felt that it was heading for catastrophe and that the country was far from being successful. He could not see that it had any real independence, meaning economic independence, because there was no local industry (no capital and no savings) and he thought that Senegal could not go on industrializing for ever with the help of foreign capital. Senghor was criticized because he allowed that to go on, but the people who criticized him did nothing practical to deal with the situation. The Senegalese civil servants were living examples of anti-national behaviour. Every time a civil servant bought a car, he said, he alienated his country. And they then tried to ask the people to save, although it was the civil servants who were wrecking the régime and the country. He strongly criticized the role played by the one political party. The party's only function was to get in membership fees. The only part played by the district chief was to act as intermediary to the government and to exploit the people of the district. He made the people pay for a plot of land.

Mr A thought that the ordinary people were not well enough informed.

He even wondered whether the people were not deliberately kept in this condition. They were systematically offered entertainment such as sports events and pop broadcasts but he asked what was really being done for the people at large in Senegal.

There was the Dakar set made up of the top civil servants and people with money who lived without paying any attention to Africa. They all had a very great contempt for the up-country people, an ethnic contempt which led to the Wolof as a whole thinking they were the élite of the country.

Well [said Mr A], I think it is the Wolof who are sinking Senegal. I don't understand how the President, who is a Serer, can accept the values and behaviour of an ethnic group which is not his own and which is having a harmful influence.

If the Serer had been in charge of this country, I'm convinced that the present situation would be quite different [continued Mr A]. Among the Diola, too, the values which really matter are work and responsibility.

What count with the Wolof are the externals of life, the outside of people, something which is quite artificial and has no reality—just the outward appearance.

These people throw all their money away on outward show while, at the same time, people on the River or in the Diola country are dying of hunger.

Mr A thought it was scandalous to hear such things on the wireless as: 'Go and buy your Christmas silk suit a Raoul Daubry's', and even more scandalous to hear a community development officer saying that he was going to buy two. What did these people think was reality? They had no sense of reality at all.

Mr A was on good terms with all the people working with him. He refused to use the term 'subordinates' and said he had always been satisfied with the people working with him.

He had had a Tukulor cook for ten years but had never called him 'boy' and did not use a bell to summon him. He had always trusted those working with him and had given them responsibility. If things did not go right, he would tell them so in private; that, he felt, was very important.

He had always thought that the Senegalese represented a culture different from his own, but a culture nevertheless. He said that this opinion was by no means shared by all French people in Senegal. He thought that the various ethnic groups in Senegal represented the result of people's adaptation to living conditions and that, generally speaking, they had managed to meet requirements. He told us about a night watchman at a school in Senegal who kept watch with a bow and arrow and who could not read nor write, but for whom he had always felt great friendship. He possessed a humanity which Mr A respected and he said that, if he went to the night-watchman's house, he would be received like a brother and that even if the watchman had nothing to eat he would go and borrow something to entertain Mr A. He had found generosity in Senegal and that, he thought, was what really mattered, whereas in France, his own country, egotism and individualism were rife. He said the night-watchman had given his [Mr A's] name to one of his children as a sign of friendship. He did not see them as black people and had never thought of people as black. (What was scandalous, in his view, were the claims made for Negritude, Africanity and cultural originality. Such claims were constantly made in speech.) What was the ideal of the Senegalese élites, he asked? It was to be like the European in everything. That was Senegal's Vanity Fair. In fact, the ones who talked like that were the Wolofs, because the Serer and the Diola were not like that.

He cited the example of a village which was trying to make a place for itself in the Senegalese economy: it was a village which was going to build its own road for itself. It had already contributed 800,000 francs from what it earned from fishing (a very commonly accepted form of saving by the community). This five-mile-long stretch of road would take them to the main asphalt road and they looked upon this as a challenge. Mr A continued:

The Senegalese virtues can be seen here, but you don't find them among the talkers in Dakar. These people are going to supply forty men and ten women a day in order to build the road and it's going to take a long while.

He said that when he went to this village and saw what was happening, he felt confident and was happy. He hated the civil servants, who were parasites at all levels. In the first place, there were too many of them for the work they would normally have to do.

They say it's the heritage of colonialism . . . . I don't think that is any excuse. The civil servants receive a considerable share of the national income, quite disproportionate to the part they play in the nation's life.

Who are the people who matter in this country? The producers. Look at what happened in the Soviet Union: the producer was rewarded. I think it would be natural to give importance and honour to someone who produces rather than to a civil servant. It's the peasants who ought to serve as the model and not the civil servants who, for their part, are wrecking the country.

Mr A voiced his opinion everywhere at the risk of dismissal, and what he said was very ill-received by the civil servants, who lived in their exclusive little set and didn't understand, saying that it wasn't true.

The civil servants in the Information Department don't know anything at all. The people in Dakar despise those who live up-country. The Wolof at Ziguinchor College called the village women shorn-heads. Those Wolof thought themselves part of a very superior culture.

It happens [he said] that I've spent fourteen years of my life here; that's why I speak like I do. I think that this country is full of possibilities but that the civil servants ought to be thrown out. Development is bound up with the education of the people at large. Well, this isn't a project, it has been a practical reality here for a long time. It's a fact in all societies that there are people who provide models just because of their status.

Society has a practical educational influence infinitely stronger than we do. The 'take-off' will come about only when the ideological 'take-off' has been achieved among the people who provide models in Senegal. Apart from that, it's all academic. . . .

'One people, one aim, one faith.' But is there one single people in Senegal? Is there one single aim? And has Senegal one faith? What is the state of faith in Senegal? What faith? [Mr A realizes that in France, 'liberty, equality and fraternity' are empty words but he thinks that, in France, theory and practice do not have to go together. In Senegal, however, strict ideological application in practical affairs ought to be an absolute necessity.] Senegal ought to live in austerity and all Senegalese should live with each other and for each other. But in fact [said Mr A], a part of society which lives very largely in opulence, or near-opulence, on other people's labour, is failing in its calling by compromising the progress of Senegal. One can only condemn this state of affairs.

Mr A would like the Cape Verde peninsula to be submerged. He never spoke about the Senegalese as such, and distinguished the Wolof from all the other ethnic groups.

Speaking about African tourism, Mr A thought that Senegal was 75 per cent desert. From the domestic standpoint, tourism just was not part of the Senegalese way of life; and it was not competitive in the world market. Corée and Casamance, which were the only places for tourist activity, besides the fishing at the Espadon of Gorée, were not competitive as regards either the catch or the cost. Mr A did not have any faith in the Niokolo Koba scheme, which he did not think sound.

He had never had any conflict with the Senegalese but had been put off in his attempts to establish friendly relations with his Senegalese colleagues at work. He had invited them to his house, given the children presents and made numerous advances but had found nobody interested.

I don't think that modernity means having a car and a refrigerator. People are still caught between the demands of tradition (intellectuals say that they have to go to visit their aunts at least three times a week) and the need for modernization.

I am not interested in art because there are other things much more important here at the moment. As a teacher who is interested in African literature, I like Birago Diop, the films of Ousmane Sembene, and Edou Corréa's column in *Dakar-Matin*.

(He read *Le Monde* and *Le Nouvel Observateur*.) He thought that co-operation was good in principle and was only right and should be kept on, but that assistance should be put to better use. In reply to the question whether he would let his son marry an African girl, he said that he wouldn't mind, provided she wasn't a Wolof. . . .

Interview with Mr C

Mr C was aged 39, a teacher who had spent eight years in Senegal after living two years in Upper Volta. He had elected to come to Senegal for the sake of adventure, to do something useful, because life there was easier and the climate better. He was going back to France for good because he had the feeling that interesting things were going to happen and he wanted to take part, and he was also going back because of his children. He thought that a change was necessary after a certain time.

He was disappointed because no one made enough effort at any level. There was no attempt at financial discipline and not enough demands were made on the civil servants and young people.

The economic situation isn't splendid. The country could get on, provided that there was a very firm policy as regards economically profitable investments. I don't see very well what the Senegalese could do. They're not managing too badly. They're using European methods but they rely too much on foreign capital and not enough on human investments.

I'm often in agreement with what Senghor says but it doesn't get further than words. Trade unionism is considered here as a safeguard and not a fight. There's no militant spirit and no spirit of social struggle. African socialism is just a word. They're on to a good racket.

Senegalese tourism is very badly organized but it has possibilities. Senegal has the advantage of being very well situated. These possibilities ought to be exploited. They ought to go in for popular tourism and not luxury-class tourism (Casamance).

I have no real contacts with the Senegalese. I haven't any Senegalese friends except people in the UPA, the teaching union. I haven't had any time and besides, it's difficult. A few pupils or former pupils come to see me, for a drink or lunch, but that's the beginning and end of it. We talk about work. It's not easy to make friends.

I haven't got any opinion about mixed couples, that's their business. You don't see many of them. You don't, for example, see a white man with a black wife. We don't know them well enough.

If my daughter were to marry a black? I don't know at all how I would react. We haven't reached that stage yet.

I have never had any trouble or conflicts with the Senegalese. Politics, co-operation, technical assistance? Co-operation is good in principle but there's more a neo-colonialist attitude behind it. It doesn't work too badly. The chaps do their stuff. What shocks me is that those working on the co-operation programme are thought of as second-class citizens. They are useful and they ought to be listened to. They ought to have the right to join a trade union and to demonstrate. The only right they have is to keep quiet. This is true both on the aid and co-operation side and on that of the Senegalese Government. It is also one of the reasons why I'm going. You're condemned to stay silent. They ask pupils, the messengers and the few African teachers that there are for their opinions and we are the last ones to be concerned. The French who are working in industry are represented on the Economic and Social Council but we have no representation. That's a form of discrimination which I don't think is right for foreign workers in France and I don't think it right here, either.

The Administrative Building is Senegal's biggest dormitory. I seldom go there because you waste your time there like you do at the French Consulate. You always have to revert to administration by force. Only the heads of departments work, maybe, and all the rest are just a joke. The Senegalese haven't any idea of saving and you can hardly give them money to look after. I found this out at the UPA. You can never find out where the money goes: it's what they do in their spare time. There are leaks everywhere. It has a good side because, when there is some money, everybody reaps the benefit from it but it goes completely out of our control. Their view is that when there is some money, everyone should profit from it.

Among the chief qualities of the Senegalese you have to mention their kindness, their sense of hospitality and their fellow-feeling for each other. Their great defect comes from their lack of exactitude and discipline. In addition, their fellow-feeling turns to parasitism and their kindness makes them too indulgent towards friends, cousins, and friends of friends. They also have a sense of decorum and they like show. They certainly like fine clothes and flashy cars. It's a very mediaeval attitude which isn't peculiar to Africa but it's more open here and more striking because there's such very great social inequality. Talk here is something exasperating, particularly the pleasure they take in showing off when they speak. The decisions taken are just so many words. They take a decision and then they think that all their problems are solved. Words have a magic power and often relieve you from going on to put your schemes into practice.

I know very little about art and culture but I think they have some very interesting things in these fields. What I do know seems to me very interesting, particularly in sculpture and literature. There's a special sensitivity about it which deserves to be more widely known.

Interview with Mrs E

Mrs E was 32 and had no profession.

I've been in Senegal for fourteen years. I came with my parents when I was 18. Life is easier here than in Paris, where I should like to live. I am very happy here in Senegal. I don't belong to any clubs. I haven't travelled very much in Senegal and I haven't any precise opinion about the different races in Senegal.

Having come to Senegal when young, nothing astonished or exasperated her. She felt perfectly adapted. Even if things didn't go very well, it didn't matter very much.

I'm not very exacting over details. I find the Senegalese likeable. I get a lot of ideas from outside. I think one has to be honest. I hope they get out of their difficulties but it will be hard. It will take three or four generations for them to do this and for them to be on their own, without assistance, with a very strong, authoritarian régime, in a nutshell, a Mao-like régime. You mustn't always tell people that they won't manage. That's very bad. You must trust them.

The Muslim faith plays a very important part. Hospitality, fellow-feeling and kindness are the characteristics of the Senegalese.

The university students are pleasant but outside the university I don't know them. I don't invite them home. I live on the edge of African society in Senegal. There are no conflicts between us and I've never had any problems with them. We simply don't have much to do with each other. I would certainly like to know them a little more.

I discovered ancient Negro art at the World Festival of Negro Arts. I was amazed because I didn't know anything at all about it.

I know very little about African films and nothing at all about literature.

Conclusions

Ethnic peace and racial tensions in Senegal

Our survey confirmed the view that the ethnic groups which make up present-day Senegal (principally the Wolof, the Serer, the Lébou, the Tukulor, the Fulani, the Mandingo, as well as the Diola and other people from Casamance) get on well with each other.

Something of the ethnocentric exclusivity of former times certainly still remains in people's attitudes but these traces are diminishing daily and giving way to a Senegalese national feeling which has become the dominant psycho-social and political factor. That is why we speak of ethnic peace in describing the present situation.

On the other hand, the relations between the black African Senegalese and the marginal elements of society (e.g. the Moors, the Cape Verde metis and the Eurafricans) and the foreign residents (e.g. the Lebanese and French) give rise to certain tensions. These tensions are probably not causing interracial conflicts at the moment and one is justified in speaking of interracial peace in Senegal. This peace, however, is not of the same quality as the inter-ethnic peace which we have just mentioned.

Basically, Senegal is still in the grip of the post-colonial situation which it has in common with other developing countries. This being so, one can see why the whites are thought of by the Senegalese as a whole as foreign elements whose activities, attitudes and fate are inseparable from the former colonial power. Here recent history has a strong influence on the present.

Whether the Senegalese think that they need technical assistance from the whites or whether they think they can do without it, tension inevitably creeps into their relations with them.

97

The Lebanese, who are closer to the Senegalese because they frequently speak Wolof and because certain of them are Muslims by religion, are nevertheless foreign elements too, thought of as such and conscious of being such.

As for the Moors and the metis, they are marginal elements precisely because they, as it were, oscillate between the Senegalese at large and the foreign Arab and European elements. There are thus tensions, if not conflicts, between these marginal elements and the majority of the people in the country.

The commercial competition which sets the Senegalese against the Moors, the Lebanese and the French nourishes these mutual feelings of hostility.

Ethnocentric images within the Senegalese nation

In spite of the interaction between them, the phenomena of public life should be distinguished from those of private life. In public life, the Senegalese are not seriously affected by ethnic tensions. As certain of our informants remarked or demonstrated, religion or political allegiances play a much more important part in present-day Senegal than ethnic differences. In private life, on the other hand, more notice is taken of the ethnic group. It is at this level that the traditional stereotypes continue to be of some importance.

The dominant fact, as revealed by our survey, is the sentimental attachment which everybody feels towards the ethnic group to which he or she belongs. When the Wolof speak about the Wolof, the Serer about the Serer and the Tukulor about the Tukulor, etc., they depict them and, consequently, themselves in a very favourable light. Each one attributes to his own ethnic group the virtues of intelligence, sensitivity and will-power.

A certain ethnocentrism thus persists despite the progress made in national feeling. The Senegalese in this respect are no different from the other peoples of Africa, Asia, Europe or America.

This ethnocentrism was even more obvious when the people we talked to were speaking about other ethnic groups. It was then clear that stereotypes going back a very long way still persist.

Among the Wolof, the Tukulor have the reputation of being good Muslims, and yet thieves on occasion, whilst the Serer are considered to be both hard-working and cunning, and the Diola are thought of as industrious people but forming a community which 'keeps itself to itself'. Furthermore, the Wolof regard people of the Mandingo family (Socé, Sarakolé, etc.) as honest but somewhat backward.

The Wolof themselves have the reputation among the other races of being too materialistic in outlook, too keen on money and of being conceited and arrogant as well. On the other hand, the non-Wolof ethnic groups are somewhat less critical of one another, as though their aggressivity were essentially crystallized around the Wolof.

All these stereotypes have their foundation in long past or relatively recent situations. There was, for instance, opposition in former times between sedentary farming peoples like the Wolof and nomadic herdsmen like the Fulani. The accusation of theft was made quite naturally by the sedentary farmer against the nomad, who responded with a certain contempt.

The Wolof have gradually come to be thought of principally as town-dwellers, although the majority have remained in the country. For the Serer, Diola and Tukulor, however, who until lately were exclusively country-dwellers, the Wolof of St Louis and Dakar were townsfolk: hence, the accusations of arrogance and unreliability.

Faced with the dominant urban situation of the Wolof, the others have reacted by criticizing them and by being lenient to each other. It is noteworthy that the tradition of teasing kinships between the Tukulor and Serer and between the Diola and Serer is still reflected in favourable or indulgent judgements on each other.

Islam and subsequently modernization have weakened the ethnic antagonisms of former times. For the Wolof, Tukulor and Mandingo, who are almost all Moslem, religious unity causes ethnic differences to disappear. Marriages between people of different ethnic groups are all the easier since Islam includes them all.

The increasing Islamization of the Serer and Diola is leading in the same direction and the social and intellectual successes of members of these two ethnic groups tend to remove the preconceived idea of their alleged backwardness.

The fact that a certain number of Serer and Diola belong to the Christian faith, and the survival of traditional elements of African religion, have become much more important in the eyes of the

99

Muslim Wolof than the question of the ethnic group to which people belong. This causes no religious tensions in public life but, in family life, slows down the progress of inter-ethnic marriages.

The same could be said, among the Tukulor, Wolof, Serer and Mandingo, about the persistence of castes and the prejudices going with them. These differences of caste, in fact, although they now have scarcely any significance in public life, including political life still have all their exclusive force in private and family life, preventing marriages between one caste and another.

In everyday life, the stereotypes which the ethnic groups of Senegal hold about each other still serve as reference points in inter-personal relations. Other reference points are also used, however such as religion and profession and, finally, the individual's own character. It is now untrue to say that the African exists only through and in his ethnic group, because nation-building and modern individualization are continually and increasingly making group membership less sharply defined.

It all looks as though the Senegalese, well aware of their nationhood and the Pan-African environment, take pleasure in listing sometimes humorously, their original ethnic differences.

To accuse the Fulani of a tendency to thieving or the Wolof of being rapacious is already, today, a sort of joke. The old stereotype are both admitted and rejected. They are used playfully rather than in any real group aggressiveness.

Everything leads us to think that inter-ethnic clashes have been a thing of the past for some time now in Senegal.

Racial tensions and the post-colonial situation

The distinguishing feature of the post-colonial situation is, of course that the peoples concerned are not masters, or not yet sufficiently masters, of their economy and of various technical and cultural aspects of their collective life. This situation is fraught with frustration and, consequently, with possibilities of agressiveness.

In Senegal, for example, small businesses are partly in the hand of the Moors, while medium-sized and big businesses are very largely controlled by the French and Lebanese, who are in competition with one another. Finally, the technical assistance used by the government is mainly provided by the French who, in addition, hold strong positions in industry and banking, despite recent penetration by certain North American interests.

Despite the Senegalese tradition of African hospitality and welcome, it is understandable that aspirations for economic independence are growing, accompanied by hostility towards the marginal elements or foreigners who hold such strong positions in the country.

Where the Moors are concerned, the antagonisms which have set the Moors and Tukulor against each other in Mauritania during the past decade are common knowledge among the Senegalese. This knowledge, combined with commercial rivalry and the usual common feeling of being exploited by the Moorish shopkeepers, leads to a real state of tension. There are not, of course, overt acts of violence but it has to be acknowledged that the Moors in Senegal, even when they hold the nationality of the country, are not integrated or, at all events, not sufficiently integrated into the national community.

In a situation like this, prejudices continue to flourish: all the Moors are reputed to be dirty, grasping and guilty of sending their profits back to Mauritania.

It is, all the same, interesting to note that the old accusation that the Moors stole Senegalese children and took them back home as slaves was not made by any of our informants. The tension is thus not so much racial as economic, even if it is at times tinged with racial feeling.

The Lebanese, who have specialized in business in large numbers, and some of whom are of Senegalese nationality, are none the less excluded from the national community by many of our African informants. For their part, the Lebanese too frequently hold prejudices about the Africans which cannot be described as other than racialist. They are fearful of the Africanization of higher personnel, particularly of the higher personnel in business. They say that the Senegalese do not have the necessary ability to direct an industrial firm or a business. Some Lebanese men and women even thought they felt a sexual repulsion, or lack of attraction, towards Africans of the opposite sex.

It all seemed as though the Lebanese wished to be part of the European community while fearing to be excluded from it.

We came across similar attitudes among the metis, particularly the Eurafrican metis from St Louis. The latter frequently reject the way of life and behaviour characteristic of the Africans. Their difficulty is then that they feel themselves to be white without, however, ever being sure that they are fully accepted by European circles. Being conscious of this situation, many African Senegalese condemn the metis.

Here too, although there is no conflict, there is a failure to integrate which accentuates the marginal situation of the metis.

The position of the French must finally be examined. These French people, who, for the most part, are profoundly alien to Senegalese society, living in it but not of it, hold stereotypes about that society which were brought to light in our interviews.

They have no confidence in Senegal's future or in the possibility of the Senegalese modernizing themselves. They say they are 'disappointed' by the way the country has developed, as if they had expected to see Senegal blossom into an industrial society, although France, as is officially admitted, is not sufficiently industrialized after more than a hundred years.

Some Frenchmen disdainfully lump all Senegalese together without managing to distinguish between the different ethnic groups. Others set the 'good' Serer and the 'good' Diola against the Wolof, who are accused of every sin, following an old pattern which dates from the colonial period, when country people were preferred to townsfolk and those who practise the traditional religions or Christianity, to the Muslims.

The most striking thing was that both the conservative-seeming Frenchmen and those who said that they were revolutionaries ended up, in our interviews, by expressing the same pessimism about Senegal's future.

It is, after all, only to be expected that nationals of the old colonial power should be, in the main, historically incapable of understanding the processes followed by their former colonial subjects. Their prejudices, in the end, arise from two sorts of ignorance: ignorance of the specific African cultural quality of the Senegalese, because they think that civilization can follow only one pattern; and ignorance of the far-reaching changes at present taking place in the ways in which the people of Senegal are living and thinking.

The attitudes of the Senegalese towards the French often depend on their religion and on whether they live in the town or in the country. The Roman Catholics, for example, tend to think that technical assistance and the presence of white men will be needed for a long time to come, whereas the Muslims more often wish to set a reasonable term to these arrangements. In addition, those living in the country whom we interviewed had more faith in the beneficial effects of such assistance and the presence of the whites, whereas the town-dwellers challenged it with varying degrees of vigour.

Viewed more generally, the French are still fairly well considered as individuals typical of industrial society (skill, efficiency, punctuality, etc.) while being increasingly rejected as survivals of colonialism (racial pride, eagerness for profit, lack of sensitivity, etc.).

Senegalese society in Africa and in the world

The ethnic peace of which we have spoken justifies our saying that there are no inter-ethnic problems in Senegal, and that the emerging nation should be trusted to strengthen its unity while at the same time respecting the linguistic and cultural wealth derived from the old ethnic groups.

One problem, however, would seem to call for particular effort among the Muslims of Senegal, and that is the persistence of castes and caste prejudice. This, in our opinion, would necessitate appropriate educational and critical action calculated to improve the present situation where marriage is concerned.

Consciousness of Senegal's nationhood usually leads on towards the prospect of pan-Africanism. To feel oneself to be Senegalese is, after all, only one particular way of feeling oneself to be African. From this point of view, it is Senegal's good fortune to include certain ethnic groups which overlap its frontiers. The Fulani of Senegal are related to all the Fulani of West Africa, the Tukulor live on both sides of the Senegalese-Mauritanian frontier, the Diola and other ethnic groups from Casamance live on both sides of the frontier between Senegal and Guinea-Bissao. The Mandingo in Senegal are the brothers of those in Mali and Guinea. Finally, the Wolof live not only in Senegal but in Gambia as well.

Respect for the cultural peculiarities of the ethnic groups, within the united national society, thus not only implies respect for what has been inherited from different traditions but also opens the way to a broader view of Africa and an approach to African unity. To maintain and strengthen its ethnic peace, we feel that Senegal must adopt a certain policy of internal and external regionalization.

This same regionalization is vital with regard to the integration of the Moors. The Moors would be more satisfactorily integrated within Senegal if Senegal and Mauritania were to belong, with Guinea and Mali, to one and the same harmonious economic and political grouping. In this way, the Moors of Senegal would be able to emerge more and more from their present uncomfortable marginal situation.

The metis would end the tensions between them and the Africans by taking part unreservedly in the life of the Senegalese nation and by giving preponderance to what is African in their cultural make-up over the other ingredients. We saw, in fact, that certain metis who had married African spouses and adopted African ways were already completely accepted by the broad mass of the Senegalese.

Sooner or later, the Lebanese will have to become Africanized or to leave Senegal. A minority will certainly follow the path of Africanization but the majority will probably leave the country. Meanwhile, however, until this occurs, it would be desirable for their business activities to take the form of real technical assistance in this field. The more Lebanese capital and its profits are invested and reinvested in the country, the less tension there will be between the Lebanese community and the Senegalese people at large.

As for the French, whose numbers have steadily fallen over the last ten years, it is obvious that they will be induced to return home. To avoid tensions between them and the Senegalese from degenerating into more or less violent conflicts, it would be advisable for technical assistance—better-defined, better-distributed and improved—to be quite free of anything resembling pressure of control which could be termed neo-colonial. It would also certainly be advisable for the former colonial power to share its responsibilities for assistance with other industrial States. Diversification of foreign aid is an essential condition for the freeing of technical assistance from the constraints inherited from the colonial régime. Interracial peace in tomorrow's Senegal can very probably be achieved only by this means.

The fact that we were interviewing our informants made them more sharply aware, at least for a time, of the problems posed by inter-ethnic and interracial relations. Their replies show that all the means for solving these problems successfully exist in Senegal, either actually or potentially.

Part Two
Ethnic group relations in
the United Republic of Tanzania

Ethnicity and group relations

by Yash Ghai

One of the persistent themes in the constitutional, political and economic developments of the countries in East Africa has been racial and tribal conflicts and their resolution. The colonial situation was characterized by the treatment of the various people in the country on a communal and racial basis, so that communities rather than individuals formed the organizational or legal units. It was inevitable in a situation like this that some groups received an importance quite out of proportion to their numbers. Such a situation, however, was incompatible with the imperatives of independence. The maintenance of colonial rule does not require that the people in the territory in question constitute a nation; indeed, it is sometimes necessary to ensure that they do not constitute a nation. Thus racial and tribal distinctions are preserved, if not actually encouraged. To maintain independence in these circumstances is difficult. It is necessary to forge a feeling of common nationhood and to underplay racial and tribal differentiations. Difficult as this task is, there is another complication: colonial society was not merely based on communal distinctions, it was also at the same time an unequal society. Merely to overlook racial distinctions after independence would not necessarily produce a just society. Unless a just society is produced, there cannot be any real prospects of national integration or political stability. Yet to produce a just society out of a colonial system introduces its own tensions and dissatisfactions and can lead to the alienation of whole sections of the population. Some groups must be stripped of privileges they have enjoyed hitherto; often these groups are 'minority' groups, and so the process of producing a just society can all too easily be seen as a case of racial or tribal persecution. On the other hand, not to pursue this process can build up bitterness and frustrations, which pose a grave threat to racial harmony. In the circumstances, the tasks that confront the government of a newly independent country in Africa are difficult and delicate.

In this study, we propose to examine how Tanzania has dealt with this problem and how it has tried to bring about greater racial equality and to remove the inequalities of the past without at the same time giving rise to racial bitterness or racism. The study is divided into four parts: the first deals with the position of the Asians, the second deals with the Europeans, the third deals with inter-tribal relations, and finally a section on the economic situation and its implications for ethnic relations, for we believe that economic situation plays and will continue to play a key role in determining the relations between the various ethnic groups.

Background to the position of Asians in Tanzania

It is first, however, necessary to set out an account of the ethnic relations in the colonial Tanganyika in order to see in proper perspective the policies and trends since independence. One of the most striking features of colonial rule in East Africa was the compartmentalization of society in three or more racial groups, which was reinforced by economic, social, and political discrimination and segregation. Though Tanganyika avoided the worst excesses of this system because of her status as a mandate, and later, trust territory, it nevertheless formed the pattern of organization of the society. Thus there were separate residential areas for the different communities, whether in law or *de facto,* separate schools, hospitals, maternity homes, clubs; on the political level, the institution of separate electoral communal representation stimulated racial political parties and made racial interests inevitable as political issues. On the economic level, the compartmentalization was reinforced by (a) a racial salary structure in the public and, imitatively, in the private sector, (b) the alienation of the best agriculture land to the Europeans, (c) wide disparities in the quality and number of social and economic services provided by the government for the different races. The result of all these policies was to preserve and strengthen the political economic, and social dominance of Europeans in Tanganyika. The Asians tended to occupy the middle place in this system, while the Africans were at the bottom. For the African population the British adopted the system of indirect rule, which employed the existing tribal institutions and thus tended to reinforce tribal distinctions.

Some illustrations may now be given of the operation of the system. In 1960/61 98 per cent of the estimated population of Tanganyika were African. It is estimated that 95 per cent of the Africans were subsistence-farmers, the remainder (between 400,000 and 500,000 people) being considered wage-earners (artisans, craftsmen, technicians, professionals). At the same time, the average annual incomes were as follows: Africans £106, Asians £586, Europeans £1,550.[1] Only 42 per cent of African children were receiving primary school education, whereas almost all the Asian and European children were in primary schools. The disparity became much greater at the secondary and further education levels, where the Asians and other non-African Tanganyikans absolutely outnumbered the Africans.

In trade and commerce, the dominance of the immigrants was likewise obvious; while the Europeans dominated plantations and export–import trade, the Asians had well-nigh a monopoly of the retail and distributive trade.

In the political sphere the Africans occupied an inferior position. The first African sat on the Legislative Council only in 1945. In 1954 the British introduced some political reforms including the principle of racial parity. This was an advance on the previous system but nevertheless fell far short of a democratic system. Under racial parity the Africans, constituting about 98 per cent of the population, received only one-third of the total representatives. It is not surprising that when the Tanganyika African National Union (TANU) was first formed its membership was open to Africans only. It was not until 1961 that this was changed and then not without some internal opposition, although TANU had already achieved a record of African co-operation with other groups within Tanganyika.

After independence there were several demands from various groups for radical measures to uplift the African at the expense of the immigrant. Though the passage to independence had not been

1. See below, 'The Europeans', by Gerhart K. Grohs.

marred by serious racial conflicts, there was the danger of racism once power had passed to African hands. This would have been contrary to the beliefs and declared policy of TANU. Both these aspects are well illustrated by the debate on the new provisions for citizenship on independence which is discussed in the section on the Europeans.

The provisions for citizenship was a crucial decision for the future of immigrant communities and for the development of race relations. Under British rule there was no concept of Tanganyikan citizenship, most people being British or being British-protected persons. The question at independence was whether or not all people in Tanganyika would become Tanganyikan citizens automatically. Those Africans who considered the task of equalization and better distribution of wealth as primordial could oppose the automatic conferment of citizenship on immigrants. On the other hand many immigrants would not wish for Tanganyikan citizenship since they were unsure of their own future in independent Tanganyika and wished to retain the safety of the British or Indian passport. A compromise was proposed by the government and adopted by Parliament. Certain categories of persons born in Tanganyika, one of whose parents was also born in Tanganyika and who was British or British-protected at the time of independence, would automatically become citizens. This would include most of the Africans and significant numbers of Asians. For those who did not qualify under this clause there was the provision that most of them could opt for citizenship within two years of independence and if they were minors the decision could be made on reaching maturity. Thus, so far as the law was concerned, almost any immigrant who wished to become a citizen could become one. He could not however retain any other nationality. The citizenship provisions meant that the government was prepared to accept the immigrants as full member of the new nation and as permanent residents of Tanganyika. Many immigrants opted for citizenship and it has therefore become necessary to devise a policy of race relations which recognizes the right, on the one hand, to conditions that are fair and equal and on the other hand, to ensure that the privileged position achieved during the colonial period does not obstruct the success of nationalist policies nor the establishment of a racially just country. How this policy has been devised and operated we will examine in the following three sections.

The Asians

The term 'Asian' is here used to refer to people of Indian and Pakistani origin, who are the only significant settlers from Asia. Arabs have generally been treated separately from Indians and Pakistanis. The Asians today constitute just under 1 per cent of the total population (some 90,000). The presence of Asians in East Africa goes back a long time, though until the end of the last century significant settlement was only inside Zanzibar, in whose affairs they played a key role. The early Indian connexions with East Africa were trading, but in Zanzibar the Indians discharged certain posts in the civil service. Their penetration inland in East Africa followed the partition of the region between the British and the Germans in the 1880s. The Indians, themselves under British rule, already had considerable connexions with the East African coast, and as early British interest in East Africa was partly the result of imperial pre-occupations in India, the Indians played a key role in the British acquisition and administration of the British possessions in East Africa. Their best-known activity is the building of the Uganda Railway at the turn of the century, but the Indians also served as clerks, accountants, postal personnel, soldiers. Their other major activity was in commerce, and they carried consumer goods to the remote parts of the interior; Indian shops thus became an inevitable part of the East African landscape. They stimulated the demand for consumer goods, and encouraged the cultivation of cash crops which they bought from African farmers. They thus played a key role in the introduction of a monetary economy in the region and in the stimulation of the first African attempts at cash crops.

The Indian activity in Tanganyika, then known as German East Africa, was slower; it proved difficult to recruit Indians for service there, since the British felt some reluctance to allow Indians to work in a country they did not control themselves. Indian immigration did, however, grow steadily, both because of the proximity of Zanzibar, the seat of original settlement, and because voluntary and private immigration was neither prohibited by the British regulations and nor by the Germans, who initially welcomed immigration from any source. The Germans welcomed Indian immigration basically as a means to stimulate trade; the Indians bought local produce, thus encouraging agricultural development, and sold cheap consumer goods, 'mediating trade between the railway and the village'; they acted, as 'commercial intermediaries between European firms and the natives'; and finally, they provided skilled and semi-skilled labour at inexpensive rates. Thus encouraged, the Indian immigration increased; in 1900 there were 3,000 Indians, in 1910, 6,723, and in 1918, 9,000.

The Asian population is spread throughout the various regions of the country, though a large number live in the Eastern Region. A large majority of them live in towns, Dar es Salaam alone accounting for over 28,000 of them. The other major centres are Tanga, Mwanza, Moshi and Arusha, but there are also significant settlements in Tabora, Mbeya, Iringa, Dodoma and Lindi. The Asian community consists predominantly of two religious groups, the Hindus and the Muslims, who are divided about equally; there are also smaller communities of Sikhs, Parsees and Christians. The majority of the Muslims are Ismaili, who are as a group the most important Asian community in Tanzania. Again, there are two linguistic groups: the Punjabi speakers and the Gujerati speakers, the latter including the variation of Kutchi. A precise breakdown is not available, but on an estimate, Gujerati must constitute over 80 per cent of the community.

With the success of the Indians came opposition from the German settlers, who aspired to the trade that the Indians conducted. They brought pressure to bear on the German administration to impose restrictions on the activity of the Indians and on their further immigration. These demands were resisted initially, but in the end the administration gave in, and immigration restrictions were introduced in 1912. Well before this time the Indians had travelled to the furthest limits of the colony, and set up establishments in Tabora, Iringa and Mwanza.

The Indian influence looked like increasing with the transfer of the mandate the United Kingdom, and there was some talk that the mandate be administered by the Government of India. While nothing came of this, Indians were assured that there would be no restrictions against them, and Indian immigration was allowed once again. It was not until 1946 that Indian immigration was once again restricted, but by this time there were already about 45,000 Indians in the country. There has been no significant immigration since then, the larger present numbers being accounted for primarily by natural increase.

The early Indian activity had been in the field of commerce and administration. By 1931 this was still the case, but gradually there was some diversification; some Indians were able to invest their savings and profits from trade into plantations, and in time came to own sisal estates. Increasing attention was also paid to education, so that young Indians qualified as professionals and practised as doctors, lawyers and engineers. Some turned to industry. Thus by the time of independence there was hardly any important area of activity, except agriculture, where the Asians did not play an important role. Thus while the majority of the professionals were Asians, their major activity continued to be commerce and employment in the administration, which also constituted their major service to the country. They opened up remote parts of the country and introduced modern goods, thereby stimulating the Africans' desire for money incomes; at the same time they bought his produce and marketed it in the capital and abroad. There is little doubt that the Asians were able to achieve this by hard work and simple living. Of late, however, it is becoming obvious that while the Asian's role of a rural shopkeeper is still a useful one, he has a useful contribution to make in the middle and upper echelons of skilled manpower. His professional and commercial expertise can be harnessed to the increasing activities of the State, even if the image of the shopkeeper still persists.

It was in this situation that the Asians entered the era of independence. While the leading Asian politicians had supported the movement for independence, and their political party, the Asian Association, had entered into alliance with TANU, it can be said that the majority of the Asians faced the prospect with misgivings. While the colonial system had imposed several restrictions on their activities, they were relatively free to carry on commerce and professional practice, and had indeed achieved striking success in these spheres. Moreover many Asians associated law and order with the British administration, and feared its breakdown with their departure. They were also apprehensive for their property. The fact that the Asians had these fears, despite a relatively 'moderate' African nationalist movement, is symptomatic of the relations that existed between them and the Africans. Asians have not been popular in East Africa. Quite apart from their activity as shopkeepers and traders, in which they have been accused of exploiting and overcharging, their social behaviour has given rise to resentment. There had been remarkably few social contacts between Asians and Africans, most of the relationships between them being at the shopkeeper–customer or master–servant level, neither calculated to inspire sympathetic understanding or good fellowship. There has been arrogance and snobbery on the part of the Asians, who tended to look down on the African as an inferior being. Most of their religions have not been of the proselytizing kind, so that even religion has been a factor for isolation and exclusiveness, and so of suspicion. Furthermore, the Africans have felt that Asians do not adequately support the nationalist movement, and look upon them as collaborators with the erstwhile imperialists.

After independence, there were individuals and organizations which demanded accelerated Africanization. The trade unions in particular wanted an outright Africanization of all posts and organizations, and the replacement of Asian traders with African traders. The government, while committed to a policy of non-racialism, was convinced that special measures had to be taken to ensure that the handicaps from which the Africans had suffered hitherto should be removed, even if this meant some temporary discrimination in favour of Africans. It has, by and large, been able to carry out its own policy of race relations. In this it has been helped by the fact that TANU has been either *de facto* or *de jure* the only political party, so that racial tensions could not easily be exploited politically. Another element in the Tanzanian policy has been Tanzanian socialism, so that the replacement of Asian businessmen with Africans has not become the crucial plank in policy.

Government measures

The government took measures on a wide front to remove existing inequalities. Perhaps the most important of these was the Africanization of the public sector, which is discussed in detail in the section on Europeans. Asians were also affected by the policy, although those who were already in employment and had become citizens were to be kept on. It was also made clear that the policy was a temporary expedient and that the general aim was to build a civil service of local citizens. While the policy did lead to an acceleration in the appointment and promotion of Africans at the expense of Asians, it was brought to an end early in 1964, when the President felt that the previous imbalance had been appreciably redressed. It is difficult to say how many Asians are employed in the public sector since the statistics are no longer based on race, but on citizenship. A number of non-citizen Asians are still working in the public sector.

The other important area that the government tackled was education. We have already noticed the favourable position of the Asians in this respect. It ought, however, to be pointed out that this was not entirely due to government policy since a large part of Asian education was financed by the Asian community itself; particularly important in this respect were the schools of the Ismaili community, which were to be found in even the smallest towns throughout the country. At first most of these communal schools were only for the members of the community, but in the fifties they were opened to all, though they still retained their communal character for some years. Thus in 1959 of the 7,000 pupils in the Ismaili schools which had been opened in the three preceding years, 35 per cent were non-Ismaili Asians and only 10 per cent were Africans. However, this changed rapidly thereafter and today the African pupils predominate in all schools.

The defect with the educational system was not merely that it favoured the immigrants, but also that it was based on a principle of segregation, so that not merely the communal but also the government schools were mono-racial. The government dealt with both these defects by the integration of the educational system, so that every school was open to pupils of any age. The defect of racial imbalance was redressed by a quota system, ensuring a high percentage of places for African children in all schools. Government-aided schools were brought under the direction of the Ministry of Education to facilitate the implementation of the government's policy. Recently, Parliament has authorized the government to take over all schools in the country, in view of the importance of education in the development of the nation and in the moulding of the character and attitude of the children. It is to be hoped that the integration of schools will bring about greater racial understanding and a feeling of common citizenship. A consequence for the Asian community of the integration of schools is that their children have a much tougher time now getting into secondary school, and are no longer guaranteed a place. The Asian community has met this to some extent partly by the establishment of private schools and partly by sending children to schools overseas.

The language issue is perhaps appropriately discussed with education. It is hoped that increasing emphasis on Swahili as the national language will help in the national integration, and today all schools teach Swahili; it is, moreover, the medium of instruction in the primary schools and is intended to be so also in the secondary schools when this becomes feasible.

The encouragement given to the co-operative movement is an important feature of government policies with consequences for the Asians. It has been shown that among the earliest Asian activities were the buying and selling of African produce. It was felt that in this way the Asian acted as an unnecessary middleman, and that it would be to the farmer's advantage if the marketing could be done by a co-operative in which he had a share. Purchase other than by co-operative or marketing boards was therefore made illegal. This had an important effect on the Asian traders, for it cut out a significant source of their income, pushing them into an increased reliance on retail trade.

Some other factors might briefly be mentioned. Radio Tanzania at independence had a special programme in Hindustani; since it has no programme in tribal language, it was difficult to justify the maintenance of the Hindustani programme, and so it was abolished. Also, the government has introduced a system of national service, during which the servicemen live in camps for about five months of the two-year period. The scheme is optional for certain groups, compulsory for others. It was unlikely that many Asians would have volunteered for national service, but a number of them come under the compulsory scheme and have carried out their service. Quite apart from helping the image of the community by this evidence of commitment to the nation, the experience of the youth of various races living together in such close proximity for about five months and engaged in national tasks cannot but increase racial understanding and produce a spirit of camaraderie transcending racial differences. Following a similar policy, the government, while not banning them outright, has discouraged exclusive clubs. All clubs are now open for membership to anyone wishing to join, but there would appear not to have been any significant intermingling so far. Finally, mention may be made of the government's uncompromising attitude towards any manifestations of racial arrogance. It has not hesitated to use its powers of deportation when it has felt that individuals have acted in a racially offensive way. There is no doubt that this has had the effect of moderating behaviour and utterances in public, though of course it is too much to expect that it has led to a change of heart. Sometimes this has been resented by the immigrants, who have tended to view a deportation of any member of their community, for whatever reason, as a threat to themselves. They tend to overlook the other side of the coin: that the government disciplines its own members who indulge in racially offensive rhetoric.

The future

An evaluation of the success of the government's policy is difficult to make at this stage. To a visitor, race relations in Tanzania seem a model of harmony; there is little tension and the various races live in peace and co-operation. Whether this points to a real integration is another question. As far as the Asians are concerned, a choice has been made by many that their home is in Tanzania, where they want to stay. This is a factor of some importance. There are others, however, who have felt that they have no long-term future in this country, and have accordingly not become citizens. The distinction between citizens and non-citizens is now an important one, for the one group sees itself living and working here, the other as temporary residents, to move away when the government asks them to or when the prospects elsewhere appear to be more alluring. Our basic concern is with the citizens, even though the presence of non-citizen Asians cannot fail to complicate the problem for the former.

A large number of Asians have become citizens. Exact numbers are difficult to come by, but by 1967 over 26,000 Asians had opted to become citizens, while the applications from some others were still unprocessed. This does not give the complete picture since a larger number became citizens by the automatic operation of the law, although it is difficult to ascertain the exact figure. Well over half the Asians are citizens, while some communities have a higher percentage. Ismailis, for example, who have been urged by their leader, the Aga Khan, to identify themselves completely with the country, have taken out citizenship in large numbers, and unofficial

117

estimates put it at 90 per cent. While it is possible that people who have become citizens might leave the country at some time in the future, it is nevertheless true that few at present intend to emigrate. Consequently they have begun to make the adjustments that they feel are necessary to go on living in the country. It is doubtful if they are adequate, and even more doubtful if they are undertaken with any measure of enthusiasm.

The communal institutions have opened up schools, maternity homes, hospitals and clubs, but have hardly been integrated. At any rate they have not led to any renewed social contacts, and the blame for this state of affairs must lie as much with the Africans as with the Asians, for the former have shown no great inclination for inter-racial social contacts. In time greater integration may well come about, for the common schools, university, national service, etc., are bound to have some effect. There is less arrogance on the part of the Asians, and a clear acceptance of the political dominance of the Africans.

In politics, the Asians have made an attempt to involve them-selves in TANU, but have steered away from its internal politics. Several have joined the party, and in the rural areas they hold party offices. It is doubtful, however, if any of the young Asians think seriously in terms of a political career. The Asian politicians who are nationally well known are the ones who were committed to the African cause well before independence, and whose credentials are therefore above reproach. Certainly the general elections in 1965 showed that the electorate was less influenced by racial consider-ations than might have been supposed, three Asians and one European defeating their African rivals in overwhelmingly African constituencies. But for the future, it is likely that Asian involvement in politics will be rather superficial. The increasing emphasis of the party on socialistic ethics is bound to alienate many Asian members, or at least discourage them from seeking office, though they are by no means the only community to be so affected.

On the economic side, there have been fewer changes than looked likely a few years ago. Although the State Trading Corpor-ation is taking over imports of more and more items, much of the distributive trade is still with the Asians, and most of the retail trade is still conducted by them. Indeed a visit to an up-country town presents a picture of trading activities not much different from that

before independence. Nevertheless it is felt that the Asian participation in commerce is bound to come to an end sooner or later, and
that it is wise for them to branch out into other areas. Agriculture
has been mentioned as a possible outlet. There is still ample land,
though not all of it of the highest quality, and the government has
placed a strong emphasis on rural development. There is already
some slight move to the land among the Asians, initially to com-
plement other commercial activities. It remains to be seen whether
agriculture will provide a real outlet for the Asians. Meanwhile,
their skills as engineers, doctors, lawyers, accountants and clerks
are greatly needed in the public and private sectors.

Tanzania's experience illustrates the difficulties of dealing with
racial biases and prejudices. The country's political system is able
to control excessive racial propaganda, but racial hostility remains,
and is in evidence when both the Africans and the Asians choose to
interpret important government policies in terms of race.

In conclusion, it may be stated that while much progress has
been made in race relations, the problem of the Asians has been
shelved, rather than solved. The ethos of the Arusha Declaration
merely emphasizes this point: how are the Asians to fit into a socialist
Tanzania? Neither the pace nor the direction of integration has been
clearly established. There has been no serious disturbance of the
pre-independence way of life. The economy has been reasonably
buoyant, and few real strains have appeared in society. It may be
that more 'crises' and tensions are necessary before there will be a
clearer definition of the place of the Asians.

Tribal relations

by Paul Puritt

In this section we attempt to answer several related question of considerable significance in understanding many aspects of personal and group relations in modern Tanzania. To what does the term 'tribe' refer? What was the nature of tribal relations in pre-colonial times? How were these relations changed through the period of colonialism? And to what extent are modern tribal relations important in the immense task of social, political and economic reconstruction in post-independence and post-Arusha Tanzania?

The term 'tribe' has been used, or more precisely, misused, by most authors dealing with African social relations. The first paragraph of too many books and articles on Tanzania almost invariably includes the statement that Tanzania is made up of some 120 or so tribes. What does this mean? Are we to visualize 120 distinct cultural entities, language groups, politically autonomous societies, separate regional groupings of peoples? In his Introduction to *Tradition and Transition in East Africa,* P. H. Gulliver makes the first serious attempt to tackle this question of 'tribe' for Tanzania and its sister countries. We will return to Gulliver's definition of tribe below. But first we must comment upon the widely held misconception that tribal groups in Tanzania and elsewhere have existed in the form in which we find them today since the distant past, that they have been static groupings of peoples throughout history.

As a result of very recent work by oral historians and archaeologists, we can now see that there have always been tribal units forming, joining and breaking up; individuals and groups have had to move for various reasons, join and be incorporated into other groups, and occasionally form new groups. Tribal relations in pre-colonial times were extremely fluid. It was the process of colonialism which made tribes appear to be static, which demarcated strict boundaries, which stopped the constant drift of peoples —this for very clear political and economic reasons.

What is a tribe?

Gulliver defines a tribe as 'any group of people which is distinguished, by its members and by others, on the basis of cultural-regional criteria'. To this a temporal dimension could be added for, as already said, these discrete groups are constantly changing in composition and in their location through time. Gulliver points out that

the lists of tribes established by late colonial times are in many ways arbitrary. They had been moulded by European preconceptions and political requirements, and by the development of the African peoples' interests and activities.

To say that Tanzania is made up of 120 different tribes is thus to say very little about the realities of Tanzania at any given time, except perhaps to some extent in the late colonial period. According to Gulliver,

it is then, of course, wrong to suggest that the empirical distinction between tribe and tribe is clear and unequivocal. There can be no implication that, if we really look hard enough and carefully enough, we shall be able to determine the precise limits of each tribe, culturally and territorially. Neither now in the present, nor in some discoverable time in the past, have tribes and the tribal pattern crystallized.

However, we can still legitimately use the world 'tribe'. It does after all refer to certain realities about Tanzania and other parts of Africa. The majority of Tanzanians today feel that they belong to a tribe as well as to the modern nation. But we must bear in mind the changing nature of these groups, and the fact that the groups themselves, and the word, have been used by various people at different times for certain definite purposes: first by the people themselves in pre-colonial times as units co-operating culturally and regionally; then by the colonialists and missionaries to further their own policies; later by nationalist leaders to obtain a local base of political power; and finally by post-independence leaders as something to fight against in order to forge the unity and identity which is required of a modern nation.

Pre-colonial tribal relations

Most anthropological monographs and articles on Tanzania give some examples of the complexity of tribal relations in pre-colonial times: migration, warfare, intermarriage, adoption, fragmentation, and incorporation. To quote a single example, Marguerite Jellicoe in 'The Turu Resistance Movement'[1] says,

The Turu are historically a collection of fragmented peoples from various parts of East Africa, especially from the southwest. Partly as a result of the pattern of migration of the various broken groups after they had arrived on the Turu Plateau and in the surrounding area, there are historical links between the Turu and all the immediately adjacent peoples. With the Iramba, and especially the Isanzu immediately to the north of them, they share some clan-names, while the languages are closely related; the Mbugwe, south of Lake Manyara, are also claimed as outlying relations who share some common origins with the Turu. While there have been warlike relations with the nomadic Barabaig, a Tatog group to the north-east, there has nevertheless also been extensive intermarriage. The relationship of the Turu with the other Tatog groups to the west and northwest is more mysterious. There has been recent intermarriage and migration on both sides, but it is also possible that the immigrant Bantu-speaking peoples whose descendants now seem to form the bulk of the Turu population may have been grafted on to a previous older population of whom the Tatog are in some ways a remnant. With the Sandawe there appears to have been considerable exchange of wives as well as male migration from one area to the other, while in the south of Turu country there are lineages of Gogo and of Nyamwezi descent—the latter apparently often of Kimbu origin.

Examples of such complexity can be multiplied by almost as many tribal societies as can be identified as such in Tanzania. The Chagga are said to be composed of seventeen different tribal groups; the thirty-five Meru clans originate from more than ten sources within East Africa; the Masai belong to at least ten different tribes; the

1. *TNR*, No. 70, 1969.

Pare are a combination of the Vasu and the Gweno; the Arusha, who today number over 90,000, became a tribal society some 150 years ago, and approximately 40 per cent of them can trace their ancestry to some other tribal group; and so on down the list.

The point is made very strongly by J. E. G. Sutton in *A History of Tanzania:*[1]

A map of Tanzania a hundred years ago would show a large number of tribes and separate political units. Some were complex democratic states, others consisted of small chiefdoms or were organized into large centralized kingdoms. We should not view these various tribes and units in isolation or as water-tight compartments each with a separate history stemming from a tribal ancestor and single place of origin. Tribalist studies of this sort are pointless and unhistorical. Moreover, tribes were not static and unchanging as they have often been portrayed. All tribes were developing and interacting. Contact with neighbours both peaceful and warlike, trade with regions near and far, expansion and migration in search of new lands—all these have led to intermingling and assimilation of peoples and tribes, of cultures and ideas. Tribes have thus been formed, transformed and broken down, but the people go on [p. 1–2].

I. N. Kimambo exemplifies this phenomenon in one part of the country by saying,

The history of north-eastern Tanzania between the sixteenth and the eighteenth centuries is a story of continuous movements of people into the region; a story of expansion of the communities which were already established there; and above all, a story of revolutionary reforms which transformed the earlier political structure [p. 30].

In addition to the diversity of origins, the complexities of migrations, the new alignments of political, cultural and language groups which operate within the various tribal societies themselves, external forces complicate matters even further. Tribal relations cannot be seen in a vacuum, as if the determinants of these relations were the tribes of Tanzania alone. From earliest times, and especially by the nineteenth century, these relations were seriously inflected by external pressures. In *A History of Tanzania,* Andrew Roberts says,

. . . Tanzania became deeply involved with the outside world during the nineteenth century, above all through the spread of trade in ivory and slaves [p. 58]. . . . Yet for the historian it is perhaps more important to note

1. Edited by I. N. Kimambo and A. J. Temu (1969).

that this was a time of integration as well as disintegration. People's horizons and ambitions were rapidly expanding; and they were learning, however painfully, to live together in larger units with greater access to the material and intellectual resources of the world outside. It was during this period, after all, that Swahili began to be spoken in the interior; that people living up-country began coming down to work on the coast; that goods imported from overseas began to circulate up-country. Far more than most African countries, indeed, the Tanzania of today began to take shape during the nineteenth century, and this was due not simply to the spread of coastal influences; it was due also to the fact that so much of the country had been involved in the attempt to find new forms of political organization appropriate to this world of expanding horizons [p. 84].

Tribal relations in the colonial period

Gulliver says that 'the nineteenth-century explorers, missionaries, military officers, and early administrators used "tribe" in a general way to apply to such separate groups of people as they considered they found identified by name, culture and, where relevant, political autonomy'. He does not feel, however, that this practice was part of a deliberate policy of 'divide and rule'. It may indeed be true that the vast majority of colonial officers serving locally found it more efficient or expedient to deal with what they considered to be separate tribal units. Some officials may even have felt that they were thus helping to conserve certain historically legitimate aspects of African culture. But on even the most cursory glimpse at the effects of both direct and 'indirect' colonial rule; it must seriously be doubted that these policies were fortuitous. Gulliver admits that 'a principal threat to the unity of the modern nation-state is the existence and strength of the tribes, of tribal particularism, loyalties and alignments, and of discrimination on the basis of tribe'. And these were precisely the effects of colonial policy. From the fluid pre-colonial situation of complex interrelationships, the colonialists set up and administered separate groupings of peoples, quite often following existing cultural and regional divisions, but just as often ignoring them. With the establishment of distinct native authorities', the machinery was set in motion for the creation of particularistic vested interests which were often the major reason for the lack of a unified resistance to colonial rule, and remain even today significant obstacles to national unity.

John Iliffe in *A History of Tanzania* brings out yet another aspect of the effects of this policy.

. . . during the 1920s the British Government reorganized the system of tribal government throughout Tanganyika. Their policy of 'indirect rule' was designed to restore so far as possible the tribal institutions as they had existed before European invasion, and then gradually to adapt these institutions to the new demands of colonial rule. At first, most Tanzanians seem to have welcomed this move, which often gave them more systematic local government than they had experienced under the Germans, but gradually the system produced serious social tensions. One of the reasons for this was that by selecting the tribal leaders from 'legitimate' families the British created an officially favoured group in each tribe. This group generally acquired more and more of the benefits which came from improvement [p. 136–7].

Not only then was the colonialist policy of 'indirect rule' a deliberate policy of divide and rule in terms of freezing the existing tribal pattern and separating the tribes of Tanzania from each other, but this policy also encouraged class formation by recognizing chiefs and bureaucratic élites—a process which may yet prove to be more disruptive to African unity than tribalism.

Colonialism took different forms throughout Africa, and even within particular African countries. Successful colonialization demanded a political and social organization through which the colonialists could effectively work. Some form of centralized African chiefdom or kingdom was the usual model sought. In Uganda, for instance, Ganda society almost ideally suited British interests. Its hierarchy and bureaucracy could be manipulated, and were helped to expand in order to take in as much territory as the British wanted to exploit.

In Tanzania, however, the process was not so simple. Few very large, well-organized chiefdoms or kingdoms existed. The colonialists faced a diversity of socio-political types and had to devise various forms of manipulation. 'Divide and rule' was occasionally replaced by a policy of 'unite and rule'. Around Kilimanjaro, one of the most fertile and attractive parts of the country the seventeen Chagga 'tribes' were helped to unite under a single paramount chief, in order to ease the task of colonial administration and allow the resources of the area to be more efficiently exploited.

In Kigoma, the western region bordering on Lake Tanganyika, a different strategy was necessary. The Ha, who inhabited this area, already formed a hierarchical kingdom through which the colonialists presumably could effectively rule, but the great distance from the export centres demanded unusual tactics. Cash cropping was outlawed, and taxes were collected by forcing young men to become labour migrants on the sisal plantations near the Indian Ocean coast and the cotton-fields by the shores of Lake Victoria. Such migrations of adult males are still a serious obstacle to development in Kigoma.

Other societies (such as the Masai, whose socio-political organization was so decentralized and alien to the colonialists that they were often allowed to rusticate) were simply ignored, and treated as live museums for the amusement of European settlers and tourists. However, if they occupied fertile land in economically viable areas, they could not be left untouched. As in the Arusha case, centralized institutions were imposed, e.g. chiefs who had no legitimacy in the eyes of the people, but who nevertheless provided a means through which the colonialists could rule more effectively.

These different attitudes had significant results. The kinds of movements of people which characterized pre-colonial times changed. Certain areas obtained an advantage over others through their earlier access to capitalist development. Where colonialists chose to make the effort, administrative and economic structures were created. Mission schools provided some education for a small proportion of the indigenous African population.

In a sense, this can be seen as a continuation, rather than an interruption, of pre-colonial organization. Societies which already had a degree of centralization and were themselves prepared to conquer and annex were often those which collaborated in the colonialist development enterprises. Their leaders received the early benefit of Western education, literacy and skills in the budding capitalist economy. Schools for the sons of chiefs were created. Councils of chiefs were invited to play a minor role in the governing of the colonial territory. As capitalist institutions began to take root, and ships laden with the raw material of Tanzania left the ports of Dar es Salaam and Tanga for the 'mother country', a few indigenous groups continued to entrench their power and interests in the developing areas.

The post-colonial period

It was this panorama of unequal development which Julius Nyerere and the Tanzanian African National Union (TANU) inherited after the declaration of political independence in 1961. With liberal, democratic idealism, Nyerere almost immediately moved to abolish the council of chiefs and began the attempt to distribute the development effort more equally throughout the country. The shortage of trained people, however, severely limited the possibilities. The personnel needed in government, in the economy, and in education had to be recruited from the Tanzanian élite, most of whom had vested local interests; to this day, members of tribal groups from the areas which had mission education and the earliest access to colonialist, capitalist enterprises, seem to be disproportionately represented, i.e. among the Chagga, Haya, Sukuma and Nyakyusa

Seeing the inherent dangers, Nyerere undertook the creation of a national ethic; for an amorphous entity, with artificial boundaries, its people operating within tribal units as a result of the 'false consciousness' that was part of the colonial heritage, could not survive unless Tanzanians co-operated as Tanzanians. But once established, institutions which bring profits to a few but control national political and economic machinery are tenacious. Even urbanization, which weakens the importance of territory as a factor enhancing tribal interests, did not solve the problem. In the cities and towns, tribalism survives in ethnic group relations; members of ethnic groups maintain their ties with the tribal homeland through the ownership of land and houses, through wives, extended families or ideological connexions.

Under normal capitalist processes, investment would continue to flow mainly into the areas which were already to some extent developed; this would obviously happen at the expense of the poorer, neglected parts of the country. After the Arusha Declaration of 1967, a more equitable distribution of development effort was attempted, and Masailand, Dodoma and Kigoma, for example, which have a tremendous potential for livestock and agricultural expansion, have become the objects of government attention.

One of the most significant steps towards securing a new alignment of rural groups and their allegiances has been the creation of *ujamaa* (socialist) villages throughout the country. It is difficult to say exactly how many, because the President's paper,

Socialism and Rural Development, has been very differently interpreted by different people. On a very strict definition there may be less than 200 true *ujamaa* villages, but new villages of one kind or another probably number some 2,000.

The villages are an essential part of the policy of providing new social and economic institutions among the rural population and opening up new land. This, however, will not in itself change tribal relations: only a few *ujamaa* villages have a population drawn from more than one tribal group, the vast majority are inhabited by people of the same tribe.

These new villages are essential if agricultural productivity is to be increased. It is equally necessary that they should provide the means of inducing the rural population to abandon tribal allegiances and vested interests. Given the present strength of tribal bonds and the antagonism between tribes, on what other basis can segments of the rural populace be expected to pack up and move from their homeland to another part of the country? The challenge of establishing a new village is enormous enough without the added hardship of losing the feeling of belonging which is still an ideological touchstone for even the poorest members of any tribe.

However, people rarely move to new locations in any country without following kinship or ethnic lines. In the short run this will also be the pattern for *ujamaa* villages, but, as the tribal members grow attached to the land of their *ujamaa* village, their identity with the tribal homeland will inevitably weaken and finally disappear. Active and sympathetic central government involvement with *ujamaa* villages should then lead to a stronger concern with the national aspects of development. The time dimension, referred to earlier in a definition of tribe, will also help to bring about a new fluidity in group relationship and end the static phase of tribal relations in Tanzania.

Conclusion

There are, then, good social, scientific and nation-building reasons for not using 'tribe' as a unit of analysis. This is true not simply because we are unhappy or uncomfortable with the word in the political climate of the 1970s: it likewise takes account of the objective fact that the majority of Tanzanians still consider themselves to be members of a tribe and live their daily lives with a strong sense of tribal allegiance. This is a phase through which the people of Tanzania will pass. National development should do the rest; expanded education and better communications will hasten the disappearance of this phase of static, parochial tribal relations.[1]

Taking the long view, seeing group relations from pre-colonial to post-colonial times, we must find more useful categories for the purpose than tribes.

One such basis lies in the different ways in which people make a living, as this in turn largely determines socio-cultural structures. We have hunters and gatherers (or foragers) such as the Hadza; pastoral peoples such as the Masai; mixed farmers like the Sukuma and Arusha; and farmers, like the Chagga, Meru, Myakusa and Haya. Each of these socio-cultural groups is in interaction with the others partly through proximity, partly because of the needs of their internal economies. Those with an expanding agriculture and some degree of political centralization best suited the requirements of the colonialists; the smaller, decentralized societies were largely neglected, the more centralized provided men and raw materials for the colonial capitalist economy. Wherever Tanzanians had a share in political and economic institutions, it was the élite of these few societies who occupied the key positions. 'Tribal' relations must always be seen in terms of this incipient social class formation which determined the roles of individuals, groups and tribes in society.

1. We have not concerned ourselves with the problem of language in this section. It should be noted, however, that the Swahili language has played an enormous role in breaking down tribal barriers. Swahili is now variously spoken and understood by approximately 90 per cent of Tanzanians. (See Wilfred Whiteley, *Swahili: The Rise of a National Language,* 1969.)

The Europeans

by Gerhart K. Grohs

The literature on ethnic and racial groups in Tanzania contains very little about Europeans. Angela Molnos said in 1965 that the statement made in the report of the East African Institute of Social Research was still valid ten years later: 'The position of the European community also requires investigation since there is little knowledge of their social and economic role in East Africa and of their ties with their countries of origin.'[1] Hence the remark: 'The Europeans are the most unexplored tribe in Tanzania.'

The period up to independence

Numbers of Europeans. The first Europeans who came to Tanzania in fairly large numbers in the nineteenth century were German. In 1894 there were 750 Germans in German East Africa. By 1900 the numbers had increased to 1,139. From 1894 up to the First World War the figures were as follows:[2] 1894, 750; 1900, 1,139; 1905, 1,873; 1911, 4,026; 1914, 5,663.

After the war, the British started to replace the repatriated German officials and settlers in what had now become a British Trust Territory. The economic crisis of the 1930s temporarily slowed down the increase in the numbers of Europeans, but the

1. Angela Molnos, 'Die sozialwissenschaftliche Erforschung Ostafrikas 1954–1963', *Ostafrika*, p. 83, Berlin, 1965.
2. Figures from: Ernst Weigt, *Europäer in Ostafrika. Klimabedingungen und Wirtschaftsgrundlagen*, p. 48, Köln, 1955.

total nevertheless continued to grow:[1] 1921, 2,447; 1926, 4,200; 1931, 7,989; 1938, 9,165.

Compared with its neighbour, Kenya, which had 20,894 Europeans in 1938, Tanganyika (as it then was called) had relatively few Europeans. More nations were represented too, among the Europeans, than in other British territories. A 1934 report by the British Government to the League of Nations[2] indicates that there were 8,228 Europeans, from the following countries of origin (only nationalities with over seventy-five members were counted): United Kingdom, 4,011; Germany, 2,149; Greece, 918; Switzerland, 220; France, 199; Italy, 150; Netherlands, 141; Belgium, 98.

This variety had further accentuated by 1969.

The Second World War caused another exodus of Germans. The 1944 figures, the first available after 1938, showed more Europeans, partly military personnel, and refugees (especially from Greece and Poland). In 1948, the total fell to 10,468 (not including Poles living in refugee camps and some—mainly Italian—army personnel).[3] The next figure (1952) showed an increase to 17,885, a trend confirmed in the national census of 1957, and reversed by 1967.[4]

Geographical distribution, occupations. Four regions (North, East, Southern Highlands, and Tanga) contain 45 per cent of the territory, but included 77 per cent of the Europeans in 1952.[5]

Although the government and administration were concentrated in Dar es Salaam, only 3,603 Europeans lived there in 1952.[6] Hence the European minority was much less physically evident than in Nairobi which, in 1948, had six times as many Europeans as Dar es Salaam. Only 32 per cent of the Europeans lived in towns in 1934, and only 23 per cent by 1948.[7] After Dar es Salaam,

1. Weigt, op. cit., p. 48.
2. *Report by H.M. Government ... to the Council of the League of Nations on the Administration of Tanganyika 1934,* p. 121, London, HMSO, 1934. Also quoted in: Adolfo C. Mascarenhas, *Urban Development in Dar es Salaam,* p. 53, Los Angeles, Calif., University College of Los Angeles, 1966 (unpublished thesis).
3. Weigt, op. cit., p. 49.
4. The East African Statistical Department, *Tanganyika Population Census 1957,* Nairobi, 1958. *Monthly Statistical Bulletin.*
5. Weigt, op. cit.
6. ibid., p. 58.
7. ibid., p. 70.

TABLE 1. Occupational structure of the European minority

Occupation	Tanganyika (1931)	Kenya (1938)
	%	%
Agriculture	24	24
Administration	24	12
Trade	10	24
Professions	16	15
Handicrafts, industry, etc.	16	17
Transport, etc.	10	8

Source: Weigt, op. cit., p. 74.

Arusha had the highest percentage of Europeans (cooler climate, plantations, flourishing industries). The usual pattern of Europeans concentrated in the cities did not apply. This is reflected in the occupational structure of the European minority, as a comparison with Kenya shows (Table 1).

There were more Europeans engaged in administration than in Kenya but far less in trade, because trade in Tanganyika was handled almost exclusively by Asians. The European population was less permanent than in Kenya, as the administrators returned home after they had served their term. There were 2,747 (16 per cent) civil servants in Tanganyika in 1952, and 3,134 (9 per cent) in Kenya in 1950. In 1952, one-fifth of the male Europeans were missionaries (1,378 Roman Catholic and 606 others).

Table 2 gives further occupational details, for 1952.

TABLE 2. Occupational structure of the European minority

Occupation	Men	Women
Independent	952	137
(Employer)	(596)	(68)
Employees	6,213	1,935
(State service)	(2,008)	(573)
Unemployed	5	—
Not known	470	537
TOTAL WORKING	7,640	2,609
Housewives	—	3,179
Children under 14	2,183	2,106
TOTAL POPULATION	9,947	7,938

Source: Weigt, op. cit., p. 79.

Economic problems. Land policies, which created many tensions between Europeans and Africans in other countries, did so to a much lesser extent in Tanganyika. The German Government alienated 1,922,700 acres (most of which was sold by auction to settlers). In 1924, another 1,700 acres in the South, and in 1926, 40,000 acres in the Iringa district, were given to non-Africans. By 1951, only 1 per cent of the total area was held by non-Africans. In 1953, the government agreed not to alienate land required for African expansion, and in 1960, shortly before independence, it decided that only under exceptional circumstances would long-term rights of occupancy be granted to non-citizens.

One reason for this cautious policy was that Tanganyika was a Trust Territory, and United Nations visiting missions were willing to hear all complaints connected with land questions.[1] On the other hand, so little land was available to European settlers that, of the 21,000 European residents in the fifties, only 3,000 could be considered as permanent.[2]

The employment picture was different. Society was stratified into three classes: Europeans at the top; Asians in retail trade and semi-skilled jobs; African peasants in agriculture or unskilled workers in the towns.

As Europeans were few, their social and financial advantages over Africans were less noticeable than those of the Asian traders and shopkeepers, although their concentration in certain quarters (e.g. Oyster Bay in Dar es Salaam) gave a certain physical and territorial expression to the economic separation of the different ethnic groups.

In 1961, the average annual salaries were: £1,546.60 (Europeans), £586.12 (Asians) and £106.20 (Africans).[3] As Mascarenhas remarked,[4] these differences did not necessarily reflect special skills or educational qualifications. The disparity in incomes and status caused African resentment of European privilege. Africanization was a strongly advocated policy of the African political party

1. cf. Thomas Patrick Melady, *The White Man's Future in Black Africa*, p. 97, New York, N.Y., 1962.
2. ibid., p. 90.
3. cf. Government of Tanganyika, Central Statistical Bureau, *Employment and Earnings in Tanganyika 1961*, p. 21, 23.
4. Mascarenhas, op. cit., p. 96.

which won independence for Tanganyika in 1961: the Tanganyika African National Union.

Political development. Soon after the Second World War a small group of Africans formed a political association, the Tanganyika African Association (TAA), which remained for many years 'the sole organization with even remote potential to represent the modern political aspirations of Africans'.[1] Its first convention was held in 1946, its second in 1948. Membership rose from 1,789 members in 1948 to 5,000 in 1951, but its links with the great majority of Africans remained very superficial.

One issue greatly sharpened political awareness: the Meru land dispute. A steady increase of the population in the Kilimanjaro area (mainly inhabited by two tribes, the Meru and the Chagga) had produced an acute land shortage.

In this fertile region, the German Government had granted freeholds to European settlers. Part of these were returned to Africans by a judgement of Justice Mark Wilson in 1946. This, however, did not greatly alleviate the pressure, and a decision of the British Government in 1950 to create a new big European area for a dairy scheme by moving 300 Meru families to a new location caused an outcry. The Arusha branch of the TAA took up the fight and brought the whole question before the United Nations Trusteeship Council, which discussed the issue three times. It then came before the Fourth (Trusteeship) Committee of the General Assembly, which requested the United Kingdom to revise the position.

Stephens rightly remarks that the Meru land case 'became a *cause célèbre* among politically conscious Africans'. It involved the two deepest fears of all Africans: economic and cultural deprivation from loss of land, and political domination by white settlers. It thus provided the potential political élite with an issue upon which they could make common cause with less politically conscious elements of the population.[2]

British policy was paternalistic, and firmly based on 'multiracialism', i.e. 'proper provision for all the main (racial) com-

1. Hugh W. Stephens, *The Political Transformation of Tanganyika: 1920–1967*, p. 67, New York, N.Y., 1968.
2. ibid., p. 85.

munities'.[1] But this multi-racialism did not mean complete equality, or the distribution of power in proportion to the number of people in each ethnic group; for example, it gave more seats in the Legislative Council to Europeans and Asians than to Africans.

The Trusteeship Council mission which came every three years recommended an increase of the African representation on the Legislative Council, and questioned the principle of 'multi-racialism' in the sense used by the government.[2] The governor in consequence appointed a committee on constitutional development, which recommended a parity formula, i.e. equal numbers of seats for Africans, Asians and Europeans. The governor accepted this recommendation. Both Europeans and Africans were dissatisfied with this solution. It was seen by some as the best device available for maintaining racial harmony, although many regarded it only as an interim solution.[3]

Underlying the dissatisfaction of a growing number of educated Africans was the economic discrimination as between Africans and Europeans. As a consequence of a recommendation of the Holmes Commission of the Civil Services of the East African Territories (1947), government salaries for Africans were only three-fifths of those paid to Europeans.[4] The Tanganyika African Government Servants Association accordingly complained to the 1951 visiting mission about low salaries, discriminatory rates of pay and the use of expatriates for supervisory posts even when qualified Africans were available.[5] These complaints affected the political relations between Europeans and Africans, and became a part of the political history of Tanganyika (and Tanzania) up to the present day.

The other major factor (constitutional development) remained important only up to independence.

It first arose when TAA protested in 1947 against the revision of proposals for a Central Legislative Assembly in East Africa, made under pressure exerted on the British Government by Kenya

1. Lord Hailey, *An African Survey* (3rd ed.), p. 194, London, 1963.
2. United Nations Trusteeship Council Visiting Mission, *Report*, p. 34–5, 1948 (T. 218).
3. Stephens, op. cit., p. 98.
4. cf. Great Britain, Commission on the Civil Services of Kenya, Tanganyika, Uganda, Zanzibar, *Report 1947–1948*, London, HMSO, 1948.
5. Stephens, op. cit., p. 105.

Europeans who wanted stronger European representation.[1] These two issues continued, in 1954, to occupy the newly founded Tanganyika African National Union (TANU), which became the dominant African political party and led Tanganyika to independence.

Julius Nyerere expressed his views on race in a paper written as a student in Edinburgh in 1952 entitled 'The Race Problem in East Africa'.[2] He openly denounced the privileges of the white minority, and the arrogance with which many of them treated Africans. But he also advocated a pluralistic Tanganyika:

> The Africans, and all the non-Africans who have chosen to make East Africa their home, are the people of East Africa, and frankly we do not want to see non-Africans treated differently, either to our advantage or disadvantage. . . . We must build up a society in which we shall belong to East Africa, and not to our racial groups, and I appeal to my fellow Africans to take the initiative in this building of a really harmonious society. . . . We appeal to all thinking Europeans and Indians to regard themselves as ordinary citizens of Tanganyika; to preach no divine right of Europeans, no divine right of Indians, and no divine right of Africans either. . . .[3]

African opinion was split on this question from the beginning. In 1958 Zuberi Mtemvu, a former provincial secretary of TANU, founded the African National Congress (ANC). In a memorandum written in the same year, Mtemvu blamed Nyerere for protecting Asian and European friends, and he opposed the idea of opening TANU to non-Africans. Mtemvu and his party were defeated in the 1960 election, but a new party—founded in 1962 by another former TANU leader, C. U. Tumbo—the People's Democratic Party (PDP), attacked Nyerere's plan for ending the separation between Europeans, Indians and Africans in the school systems as too moderate, and advocated rapid Africanization.[4] TANU remained a party open only to Africans, but it supported Asian and European candidates in the tripartite system of voting introduced by the British Government in the general elections in September 1958 and February 1959.

1. cf. Henry Bienen, *Tanzania, Party Transformation and Economic Development,* p. 28, Princeton, N.J., 1967.
2. Reprinted in: J. Nyerere, *Freedom and Unity,* p. 23–9, Dar es Salaam, 1967.
3. Nyerere, op. cit., p. 28–9.
4. Bienen, op. cit., p. 58.

Nyerere believed that, after independence, the economic basis of the race problem would be a main obstacle to the political development of Tanganyika as an independent country. He wrote in December 1959:

In this country, as in most other colonial or ex-colonial plural societies of Africa, the economic divisions between rich and poor coincide almost exactly with the divisions between the races. Wherever extreme poverty exists beside a visibly high standard of living, there is the risk of bitterness. When the problem is linked with racial differences, it is far more politically dangerous than in mono-racial societies . . . but, when independence comes, we must tackle this economic complication quickly. If we cannot close the gap rapidly enough, so that differences in economic status become less glaring and, above all, are freed from their former links with racial divisions, there is a possibility that the potential danger might become a reality, and the economic problem brings us back to the very race problem which we claim to have solved.[1]

The position of Europeans since independence

The politics of Africanization. The position of the Europeans was changed after independence by the very fact that an African government had taken over. The new government, headed by Nyerere, comprised two European ministers, D. N. M. Bryceson and Sir Evrest Vasey, and several European members of Parliament were appointed by the President, including Dr Stirling and Lady Chesham.

In 1963, on Nyerere's initiative, membership of TANU was opened, not without opposition, to European and Asian citizens. The government then started an Africanization programme. The first step was the citizenship bill which, immediately after independence, gave rise to an extensive discussion on the position of the Europeans. The bill met with strong opposition, especially in the TANU National Executive Committee. There were demands to abolish the reserved seats for minorities in the National Assembly, for more rapid Africanization of the civil service and the establishment of a Republic.[2] On 17 February 1962, the prime minister

1. Nyerere, op. cit., p. 73–4.
2. cf. Tanganyika Assembly Debate, *Hansard,* 36th Session, 5th Meeting, 17–18 September 1961, Cols. 303–20, 324–74.

announced in the National Assembly the appointment of a commission on Africanization under the chairmanship of the Hon. S. A. Maswany, Minister without Portfolio.

In a personal letter to the chairman of the commission, the prime minister laid down guiding principles, of which the most important are:

1. We wish to have a completely national civil service as soon as possible.
2. Whenever an African citizen of Tanganyika is found to be qualified and suitable for a post in the civil service, he should be offered the appointment, if necessary by displacing a non-Tanganyikan incumbent.
3. As far as possible, Africanization should progress on a broad front, but here are certain key areas and sensitive posts to which priority attention should be given. . . .
4. Any planned programme of Africanization must ensure that the senior officers of the future have a supporting staff of not less efficiency and reliability than exists at present.
5. The Commission should not examine the existing prescribed qualifications critically, in the light of the realities of our manpower resources. At the same time the greatest care should be taken that the maintenance and expansion of the services and amenities and the development of the country generally is not sacrificed by the premature appointment of Africans before they are qualified. . . .[1]

It is obvious that two principles had to be considered: (a) the greatest possible speed in Africanization and (b) the greatest efficiency of the administration. The wording of the programme made a clear decision for efficiency and against speed of Africanization if there should be a conflict between the two aims. The commission, during the first stage, recommended two features: (a) the posting of Africans to key control posts in the civil service, and (b) preference to Tanganyikans of African origin. It very carefully analysed all key posts, and made a recommendation regarding each post held by an expatriate and his replacement by an African successor. For the first year, it proposed the following,[1] for senior and middle-

1. Tanganyika, *Report of the Africanization Commission 1962,* p. 1, Dar es Salaam, Government Printer, 1963.

139

TABLE 3. Comparative employment figures for senior and middle-grade public servants

Sector	1962		1967	
	African	European	African	European
Central government	59,499	1,292	55,850	754
East African post and telecommunications	1,356	66	1,618	32
East African railways and harbours	12,898	215	11,964	91
East African community services	501	53	896	46
Local government	19,589	40	22,774	14
TOTAL	93,843	1,666	93,002	937

Source: Government of Tanganyika, Central Statistical Bureau, *Employment and Earnings in Tanganyika 1962.* Government of Tanzania, Central Statistical Bureau, *Employment and Earnings in Tanzania 1967.*

grade posts: 31 December 1961, 1,170 Africans and 3,282 non-Africans (total, 4,452); 31 December 1962, 1,821 Africans and 2,902 non-Africans (total, 4,723).

Figures are not given separately for Europeans, but progress towards Africanization was obviously made in the first year after independence.

Table 3 gives comparative figures for 1962 and 1967 for senior and middle grades, and other jobs held by Europeans and Africans.

Note that the figures list males only. Also, in 1967 the category 'African' was replaced by 'Citizens' and includes citizens of Asian origin. But this does not affect the argument.

The drop in the number of Europeans in the public services is very considerable. However, there is little increase in African employment, because the total figures remained almost the same (93,843 and 93,002). This is also a potential cause of resentment among the Africans. A comparison of the figures for employment in the private sector gives the following (with the same qualification as before with regard to the classification): in 1962, 238,396 Africans and 2,990 Europeans; in 1967, 140,228 Africans and 2,444 Europeans.

In the private sector, the pace of Africanization was thus slower, and increased rationalization of production put many Africans out of jobs. Tensions are likely to be much more acute in the private

TABLE 4. Average earnings (in Tanzanian shillings) in 1967

Sector	Private enterprises		Public sector	
	Citizens	Europeans	Citizens	Europeans
Agriculture	162	3,316	276	2,802
Mining and quarrying	325	3,778	376	2,005
Manufacturing	328	4,428	253	2,140
Construction	306	3,225	166	2,702
Public utilities	335	4,348	234	2,560
Commerce	470	4,082	—	—
Transport and communications	472	3,693	345	3,478
Services	375	2,568	355	2,647
Average	277	3,498	299	2,776

Source: Government of Tanzania, Central Statistical Bureau, *Employment and Earnings in Tanzania 1967.*

sector than in the civil service, and the official trade-union organization (NUTA) has a far more radical record than TANU itself,[1] especially on the question of income disparities as between Europeans and Africans. The situation in 1967 with regard to incomes is shown in Table 4.

It will be noted that Europeans earn more in the private sector than in the public sector, Africans less, Europeans occupying most of the top posts in the private sector. Because of unemployment, Africans may sometimes be paid even less; NUTA officials have accused some workers of accepting wages less than the minimum fixed by the government—they prefer even badly paid work to no work at all, and are prepared to assist the employer in evading the legal provisions enacted for their protection.[2]

The relative success of Africanization in the public sector has aroused criticism for the lack of progress in the industrial and agricultural sectors. As the Meru land case has shown, population pressures tend to increase resentment at the ownership of estates

1. C. K. Tumbo, former head of the Railway Works Union, was one of the most vocal critics of Nyerere in racial questions. Bienen remarked: '. . . elements within NUTA are prepared to pressure private sectors much harder than government. And some officers of NUTA's central administration are committed to a socialism much more "scientific" than Nyerere's version' (Bienen, op. cit., p. 209).
2. cf. *The Nationalist.*

by Europeans and other non-citizens. The nationalization of banks and some foreign enterprises gave some impetus to Africanization, even if the change was slow to reflect itself in employment figures. But there was no similar development at all in agriculture.

The federation of Tanganyika with Zanzibar gave a new impetus to nationalization. In Zanzibar, some Arab-owned land and enterprises were taken over by the State. Some TANU leaders wanted to know why concerns owned by Asians and Europeans were not similarly taken over in Tanganyika.

One of the main targets has been in coffee and wheat farms which are held by farmers of Dutch or South African descent; irritation is directed particularly to those who have left Tanganyika and run the farms as absentee landowners.[1]

The government had the necessary powers, having nationalized all land and abolished all freeholds. The leaseholds of a number of farms in Mbeya, Arusha and Iringa were revoked at the end of 1964.[2] Nevertheless, the position of European farmers appears stable; it seems, however, unlikely that new European farmers will be allowed to settle in Tanzania, or that expiring leaseholds will be prolonged.

1. Bienen, op. cit., p. 303-4.
2. ibid., p. 304.

Ethnic econononic differentiation

by Simon M. Mbilinyi

Background

Prior to the coming of the Western nations there were no such names as Tanganyika or Kenya. The whole coastal belt that lies north of the Zambezi River and south of the Tana River was eastern Africa. It was inhabited by groups of people which later, when Europeans came, were called 'tribes'.

Their main economic activities hinged more on nature than anything else: hunting, fishing, livestock rearing and some rudimentary agriculture, with some supporting home industries concerned with the manufacture of tools and containers. In modern terms, it was a closed economy, which took care only of individual families. As populations grew and inter-group mobility increased some limited trade took place but was confined to barter. The economy remained a subsistence economy.

The size and nature of pre-colonial agricultural activities and the state of inter-tribal trade is difficult to establish because of the absence of records. The earliest written record, *The Periplus of the Erythren Sea* written by the merchant seaman Periplus, records exports of wheat and spices from parts of the Somalia Coast, and rice, sesame oil, and honey from further south. Other crops probably grown include African arrowroot (*Tacca involucrata* Schum & Thonn), Kaffir potato (*Coleus* spp.), yam, beans (*Sphenostylis sternocapa*) and various varieties and species of root crops. Most of the crops were grown for subsistence consumption within the family household. Surpluses were exchanged either for durable goods or for other types of food within the tribe, and occasionally between tribes. The recorded exports must have constituted a very small fraction of the production.

The earliest outside contacts with the people of eastern Africa, according to written records, were people from the Middle East and the Far East. It was generally believed that the first immigrants were Arabs and Persians, in the ninth century.[1] But archaeologists now think that the Chinese arrived before the Christian era. To decide who came first is not the concern of this paper: it is what they did which matters most.

These early arrivals were mainly traders, who exchanged beads, pots and other manufactured goods for ivory, hides, skins and other items of value. They did not to any appreciable degree influence the way of life or change local economic life. Real change began with the introduction of agricultural crops and new techniques of farming. The Arabs and Persians introduced rice and rice planting in East Africa. They were followed by the Oman Arabs, who further developed rice and coconut cultivation. Minor settlements began to develop in the interior.

The cultivation of rice and coconuts was limited to the coastal areas. It is said that, save for certain favoured individuals who were allowed to grow them only for their own use, the indigenous people were not allowed to cultivate these crops. The bulk of the two crops was cultivated by slave labour on large-scale farms owned by the rich Arabs. The relationship between the two ethnic groups was that of master and slave. The masters brought in new crops and techniques of farming, but they also encouraged inter-tribal wars, and started the slave trade and all the evils that went with it.

On their way to India in the sixteenth century, the Portuguese were the first Western nation in East Africa, where they later established ports of call. To provide food for their boats they introduced oranges and pineapples to the area and a host of other fruits and cassava. It was not the interests of the Arabs, nor indeed the Portuguese, at that point, to develop eastern Africa. Although some kind of agriculture and trade had been introduced, the economic life of the indigenous people did not change very much, possibly because of the numbing effect of slavery.

1. cf. J. P. Moffet *et al., Tanganyika, a Review.*

The real change in political social and economic life in what became Tanganyika started only with the arrival of the Germans towards the end of the nineteenth century. The country was at first run by a German company. After several wars with the Arabs and others, the German Government finally took over. Social and economic change continued despite the wars. Missionaries built schools and hospitals. The government was mainly concerned with effective administration and economic expansion.

The new crops introduced and the expanded growth of then existing crops still provide the basis of the present-day economy: sisal, cotton, ceara rubber, coffee, to mention the most important. The Germans also established, in Amani, the first tropical agriculture research station, at the end of the nineteenth century. Research substations were later established along the coast and in the hinterland.

The authorities first tried to encourage plantation agriculture, but failed to attract sufficient white settlers from Europe. A later attempt to establish small-scale farmers was very successful, and was backed up by a scheme for training agricultural advisers.

All these developments were geared to production for the German market; East Africa was intended to be a tropical plantation which would supply Germany with industrial raw materials. In the process, the African became a modern peasant farmer, producing both cash and subsistence crops.

The Germans also introduced wage payments for people who had hitherto worked only as slaves on Arab estates and elsewhere.

Government investment in providing an economic infrastructure helped to develop the ports at Tanga, Dar es Salaam and Lindi, and to build railways from these ports into the hinterland.

Mining was minimal, partly because of technological limitations, partly because better-quality minerals could be got from some other parts of the world. The only minerals mentioned in records are gold, mica and limited amounts of copper.

It has been necessary to deal with the German period in some detail for the simple reason that it provided the basis of the present-day economy. When the British took over after the First World War, the economy and the administration had more or less collapsed, and the government's first priority was administrative and economic reorganization. It was necessary to speed up the change-over to a monetary economy so that the finances need to run the administration could be raised locally. The poll tax forced many people to find means and ways of getting cash.

On the whole, however, the period between the two world wars saw little real development. The British Government was not interested in spending much money on a Mandated Territory. Plans for administration, economic and social reorganization were held up by the great economic depression which started in 1929. In addition, the territory suffered the worst locust plague in its history.

It was not until after the Second World War that the British Government regained interest in the development of Tanganyika. The emphasis was once more on large-scale farming, i.e. estates or plantations. Settlers were brought in for settlements in the Highlands (Mbeya, Iringa and Arusha). The government also started the now defunct groundnut scheme under the auspices of the Overseas Food Corporation. Between 1947 and 1949 over 200,000 acres were cleared for this scheme, upon which the government spent some £34 million. Despite these efforts, plantation agriculture made no great progress, and the government turned to peasant agriculture.

In the early 1950s, local authorities bought tractors for hire to peasant farmers under a Ministry of Agriculture scheme. This scheme was also unsuccessful. At the end of the decade the accent was changed to providing more staff and funds for agricultural advisory services, infrastructure and marketing.

Finally, just before independence, a more comprehensive agriculture development policy was adopted which was continued by Tanzania during its early years. It can be summarized as follows:

1. Improving agriculture by better agricultural advisory services, working by persistent persuasion rather than by ordinances and by-laws. The farmer was free to accept or reject advice. Training centres were expanded: Tengery, Ukiriguru and Nyegezi for agriculture and veterinary officers, and two others for game and forestry.

2. Closely supervised schemes (see below); farmers who chose to participate had to follow the rules.

3. Research. Once the farmer was responding to the idea of modernized agriculture, the government arranged for research

on such items as seeds, fertilizer responses, spacing, plant
varieties, plant and animal diseases (one of the most successful
was research on cotton), and trained personnel to put the
findings into practice.
Rural people constitute over 95 per cent of Tanzania's population.
This is important in studying ethnic differentiations. In towns
economic differentiations were more visibly related to racial factors
than in the countryside.

End of the colonial period

The following is a general balance sheet for Tanzania at the close
of the colonial period in 1960:[1]
Population. Africans, 9,099,000; Asians, 177,000; Europeans,
22,000; others, 5,000.
Education. Primary schools, 3,270, pupils, 450,636; secondary
schools, 78, pupils, 14,535; technical schools, 23, pupils, 3,669;
teacher-training colleges, 32, pupils, 1,489.
Health. Government: 74 hospitals/dispensaries, 6,758 beds. Missions: 136 hospitals/dispensaries, 7,512 beds. Industrial:
31 hospitals/dispensaries, 940 beds.
Communication. Roads, 20,464 miles; railways, 1,825 miles (including sidings); harbours, 4; airports/airstrips, 51 (one international).
Gross domestic product: £185,053,000 (sterling).
Total exports/re-exports: £56,570,000 (sterling).
Total imports: £37,817,000 (sterling).

Crops and climate

Tanzania has three major climatic zones. The coast and immediate
hinterland forms a typical tropical zone, with very hot humid
weather, temperatures averaging 76° F, rainfall about 40 inches
per annum. Main crops are rubber and coconuts; both crops did
well but the climate discouraged white settlement. The central
plateau, the second major zone, has hot, dry weather, with great
daily and seasonal variations. Rainfall is uncertain from season to

---

1. cf. *Tanganyika—The Making of a Nation,* British Information Services,
1961 (RF.P.5074).

147

season. The most suitable agricultural activity is livestock rearing —not in the interest of the early colonial rulers. The mountain areas form the third zone, with a semi-temperate climate and occasional forests—an ideal climate for most of the perennia crops.

The total area of mainland Tanzania is 361,800 square miles, four times that of Great Britain. In 1960, less than 10 per cent of this land mainly in the mountain areas was under cultivation, and 1 per cent of it was foreign held.[1] Most of the settlers were British, with some Greeks, Indians and South Africans. The country is mainly open woodland, full of bush and thickets infested with tsetse flies, and it suffers from constant water shortages. The population centres are on the periphery of the country, with an obvious relation to climatic zones, i.e. the high population areas are in the Kilimanjaro/Arusha areas, West Lake, around Lake Victoria and the Mbeya/Iringa Highlands; the coast has a high population density only near the urban centres. Table 1 shows the value of cash crops grown by non-Africans and Africans in 1957.

TABLE 1. Growing of cash crops by non-Africans and by Africans (1957)

Crop	Estates		Total
	Non-African	African	
	£	£	£
Sisal	9,534,000	106,000	9,640,000
Coffee	1,300,000	7,100,000	8,400,000
Seed cotton	—	7,300,000	7,300,000
Cashew nuts	—	1,500,000	1,500,000
Groundnuts	—	1,100,000	1,100,000
Oil seeds (other than castor, e.g. sunflowers)	—	1,100,000	1,100,000
Sugar	1,000,000	—	1,000,000
Castor seed	—	900,000	900,000
Tea	773,000	—	773,000
Tobacco	461,000	188,000	649,000
Copra[1]	100,000	400,000	500,000
Pyrethrum	210,000	—	210,000
Wheat	180,000	20,000	200,000

[1] Breakdown derived by Winter and Beidelman.

Source: Winter and Beidelman, op. cit., p. 96. *Original source,* Colonial Office, 1957.

1. E. H. Winter and T. O. Beidelman. 'Tanganyika: A Study of an African Society at National and Local Levels', in: Julian H. Steward (ed.), *Contemporary Change in Traditional Societies,* Vol. 1, p. 99, Urbana, Ill., University of Illinois Press, 1967.

Education

Education was shared between the missionaries and the government. At independence, over 70 per cent of pupils were in mission schools, but these schools were unevenly distributed, as the missionaries had entrenched themselves in places where the people were responsive to their teachings and where the climate was attractive. By opening up minds, education increased needs and gave an incentive to efforts to satisfy them.

Primary education was left mainly to the local authorities, (called 'Native Authorities' in the British era and now become District Councils). As their financial resources varied, the more prosperous had more schools and better teachers, produced more educated people, who worked harder and demanded more and better economic and social facilities . . . the end result is that certain areas are way ahead of the rest of the country, both socially and economically.

Infrastructure

In the early years of German rule, the building of the infrastructure (e.g. railways) did not necessarily depend on modern-type feasibility studies. It was assumed rather that, once the facilities are provided, people will follow or even be forced to follow and make the facilities viable. In recent years, however, the emphasis has shifted to viability. The result is that roads, railways and airports primarily serve the areas which were already prosperous and could afford and support them.

Racial hierarchy

The relationship between Arabs and Africans was at first one between trading partners. It later developed into a master–slave relationship. When slavery was abolished, the Arabs remained as landlords (especially in the coastal areas, and the islands of Zanzibar and Pemba), or devoted themselves to trading. They became shopkeepers, ran small restaurants, or sold the meat from cattle and goats which they bought from farmers inland.

Most Indians in East Africa speak Gujurati, but there has been a long trade relationship between India and the coast. Indians

149

who settled along the coast and in Zanzibar largely controlled trade, and supplied capital for the Arab slave trade in the interior. As German colonization progressed inland, Indians followed in their usual role as traders. They owned the big shops (wholesale and retail), and indeed controlled, and still control, the commercial sector of the economy. Apart from the large Western companies, Asians own most of the enterprises involving a major capital outlay in the cities. Until nationalization in Tanzania in 1967, they were the main importers, exporters, industrialists and manufacturers.

The Europeans were mostly officials. Businessmen were usually agents for foreign firms; self-employed Europeans were found mainly in estate and plantation agriculture. Farmers produced cash crops for export: sisal, coffee, tea, pyrethrum and, for a short period, tobacco. European firms imported cars, machinery, chemicals and consumer durables generally, and some foodstuffs.

The economic and social hierarchy, Europeans (highest), Asians (middle) and Africans (lowest), was reflected in the patterns of residence and types of housing, business, salary structures, school, country clubs; and even in public latrines.

As the struggle for independence intensified from about 1955 onwards, many of these differences began to disappear. But the major economic differences still exist. They are examined in the next section.

Economic differences are dealt with above on the basis of area; by substituting tribe for area, the differences can be seen in ethnic terms. Economic and social differences have been accentuated by: the introduction of various crops (which depends very much on climate and topography); human development through education; the expansion of the infrastructure; the existence of towns, and relative distance from them.

Asian capitalism in Tanzania

During the period 1900 to 1914, there were about 10,000 Asians in Tanganyika: mechanics, artisans, civil servants and a few merchants. The major economic activity—mainly in European hands—was agriculture. In 1914 agricultural exports were valued at £1.5 million. At the end of the First World War, and the departure of the Germans, Asians bought up nearly all the property in Dar es

Salaam and cheaply acquired many of the former German estates. By the end of 1924 they owned 266,000 acres (against 1.5 million acres owned by Europeans).

This new economic base facilitated the expansion of the Asian community which, by 1931, numbered over 25,000. A British Government attempt to lighten Asian immigration by raising the deposits to £100 per adult plus £50 per child and dependant had little effect. From Dar es Salaam Asians moved to the interior and opened up shops which sold consumer imports and locally manufactured goods, and served as collecting centres for African agricultural produce. By 1939, it was estimated that Asian interests in Tanganyika included 17 per cent of non-African agricultural land, 90 per cent of all town property, 80 per cent of the cotton industry, 80 per cent of sisal production, 50 per cent of the import trade, 60 per cent of the export trade and 80 per cent of the transport and general service.[1]

Asians pioneered various crafts and industries: shoe-making, tailoring, tinsmithing, processing of soft drinks and foodstuffs, furniture. For a certain period, however, industry was largely dominated by European manufacturers; but in the late 1950s, Asians again began to dominate in industry. They were also prominent at managerial level. Of technical and managerial personnel in Dar es Salaam (1960/61), 42.6 per cent were Asian, 28.6 per cent were European and only 28.7 per cent were African; and 5,092 non-Africans formed the largest employer class outside the civil service and para-governmental institutions.[2]

It is estimated that the education of an Asian costs four times that of an African, one-fifth that of a European. Of some 25,000 Asian children in primary schools in 1960/61, 8,000 went on to secondary schools in Tanganyika or overseas. There were fifty-one aided Asian non-communal schools and fifty-seven communal schools. Of 514 Asians receiving higher education abroad (against 465 Africans), 335 were taking engineering, accountancy, medicine, nursing and pharmacy while the remainder were studying arts

1. George Delf, *Asians in East Africa*, p. 30, London, Oxford University Press 1963.
2. Adolfo C. Mascarenhas, *Urban Development in Dar es Salaam*, Los Angeles, Calif., University College of Los Angeles, 1966 (unpublished thesis).

and social science courses, with the major emphasis on education. A few were taking agriculture and science.

The Asians had their own clinics, hospitals and welfare centres, which they financed and staffed themselves.

They controlled 23 per cent of sisal production, grown on 420,058 Asian-owned acres (against 2.5 million European owned); over 50 per cent of the import/export business; over 80 per cent of the wholesale and retail trade; and there were over 8,000 Asians in the public service.

Thus, on the eve of independence, the Asian community had full command of its own education and its social and economic interests. Few Asians entered politics. This was understandable, in view of the community's position between the other two groups, African and European. It was not clear which would win.

The interesting question is: how and why did the Asian achieve such economic power in a country dominated—in different ways—by the other two ethnic groups?

In his book, *Black and White in East Africa,* R. C. Thurnwald gives the following reasons to explain the Asian success: (a) the simplicity of their life, a kind of economic asceticism; (b) the generally excellent family life; (c) the saving of money, which they send home to India; (d) reciprocal aid among related families; (e) Indians settle along the main lines of modern traffic (whereas Arabs stick to the old caravan routes); (f) Indians learn English and reading, writing and reckoning in Indian schools after the European fashion.

Success is also due to the Indian's industry and business acumen. They had, for example, their own banks and insurance firms. They were assigned certain economic sectors and received other forms of preferential treatment from the Europeans. Finally, they had the advantage of being a well-knit group, bound together by religious and other ties.

Government policy towards Asians

Official policy did not adversely affect the Asians. Even the control of Asian immigration had little effect in practice. However, various restrictions were imposed. Asians were forbidden to open shops in rural areas except with government permission, so that their shops were confined mainly to towns and minor settlements, i.e. planned rural areas, with a sizeable population and a trading plaza. They were also forbidden to give credit to Africans; if they did give credit, they had no redress in the courts if the borrower failed to repay. They were not allowed to canvass business in African homes or farms. They had to pay fees for land to build on in rural areas, and their licence fees were higher. The creation of marketing boards and co-operative marketing cut off a substantial amount of business. In the export trade in crops, the big Asian firms continued to compete with the big European firms.

During the early years of independence, the economic position of Asians was not affected. The aim was to create a multi-racial society in which none would be discriminated against because of colour, religion and so on. Uncertainty nevertheless persisted, and a number of non-Africans left—mostly Europeans. The Asians stayed.

Changes began to take place. In an attempt to provide education for all, all schools came under government control, and schools that were exclusive to certain racial or religious groups were directed to take students of any race or religion.

A socialist policy was adopted in 1967. After the nationalization of industries, financial institutions, import and export firms, the government in 1970 took over the whole import and wholesale trade. There were strict exchange controls. The retail trade remained as the main Asian economic activity. Asians could invest in industries referred to in the Arusha Declaration or industries now run by semi-State agencies. They also continued to invest heavily in the agricultural sector: the production and marketing of sisal, sunflower seeds, oranges, maize, millet, cattle for milk and beef, and poultry.

Asians and Europeans

Before nationalization, the European firms handled large-scale industry, the import and export of major commodities, shipping, and so on, while the Asian wholesaler and retailer was the distribution agent for most local and overseas companies. Many Asians worked for the European firms as managers, accountants and clerks.

The Europeans appreciated the shrewdness of Asians in business and found them extremely patient and hard-working as employees. There was little tension between the two groups, but practically no social mixing.

Asians and Africans

The African attitude to Asians is based on a number of beliefs:

1. Asian customs are different and peculiar. Asians keep to themselves and do not mix much with other people, and especially not with Africans.
2. In trade and employment, the Asian is a direct competitor, but has always regarded himself as a foreigner. He probably had a British passport, but holds a job which should belong to an African.
3. Asians have the further advantages of close-knit family trading relations, and many ways of obtaining financial help not open to Africans.
4. Asian shopkeepers have exploited Africans for ages but have contributed nothing directly to African welfare in return. Profits have always been sent abroad rather than invested locally.

As all schools are now open to all races, and all young people must do national service after completing their secondary education, there will be more contacts between Asians and Africans. This should help to extend and improve social relations at least between them.

The new Europeans

The original Europeans were administrators, missionaries, farmers and managers. Since independence, the numbers of European administrators and farmers have decreased. There is, however, a new influx of another type of European, the expert, who comes for two to four years, to advise the government and the semi-State agencies, or teach in institutions of higher learning. Such Europeans are regarded as people who will be only temporarily in the country, and their relations with Africans may vary from personal case to personal case.

Economic prospects and future ethnic relations

Most of this article has dealt with Tanzania as a country operating economically on Western, capitalist lines. With the Arusha Declaration and the TANU Policy on Socialism and Self-Reliance (1967), the main economic emphasis shifted to the elimination of exploitation, peasant and worker control of the major means of production, co-operative efforts, and rural development.

Nationalization has already affected large-scale industry, the large sisal estates, financial institutions, export and import firms, and wholesale distribution. The total impact will depend upon how effectively the government can assume managerial and technical control, and change the scale of values inherited from international capitalism.

In the rural areas, the emphasis is on co-operative farming and the *ujamaa* villages described above. *Ujamaa* villages should enable the government to provide schools, social services and an infrastructure faster and more cheaply; but they need good leadership, and good technicians. In certain areas good land is scarce but this could be offset by better planning and better farming. It may be more difficult to get some of the richer areas to accept the concept of the socialist village.

The future economic prospects will be largely influenced by the extent to which the people as a whole—all races and ethnic groups—are prepared to accept the principles outlined in the Arusha Declaration and subsequent documents. It is possible to be reasonably optimistic about ethnic relations: tribal feelings should diminish in importance as working and social contacts are established and extended between people from different districts and meeting through schools, national service and many other ways.

Selected bibliography

DELF, George. *Asians in East Africa*. London, Oxford University Press, 1963.

HAWKINS, H. C. G. *Wholesale and Retail Trade in Tanganyika: A Study of Distribution in East Africa, 1965*. New York, N.Y., The Economist Intelligence Unit, Frederick A. Praeger.

HOLLINGSWORTH, L. W. *The Asians of East Africa*. London, Macmillan, 1960.

MASCARENHAS, A. C. *Urban Development in Dar es Salaam*. Los Angeles, Calif., University College of Los Angeles, 1966. (Unpublished thesis.)

MBILINYI, S. M. *The Economics of Rural Development: Retrospect and Prospects*. The University of Dar es Salaam, 1968. (Mimeo.)

MOFFET, J. P. *Handbook of Tanganyika, 1958*. Dar es Salaam, Government Printer.

TANGANYIKA, GOVERNMENT OF. *Employment and Earnings in Tanganyika, 1962*.

——. MINISTRY OF AGRICULTURE, FOOD AND CO-OPERATIVES. (Various Annual Reports.) Dar es Salaam, Government Printer.

——. *The Economic Survey and Annual Plan, 1970–71*. Dar es Salaam, Government Printer.

——. *Annual Statistical Abstract 1958–1965*. Dar es Salaam, Government Printer.

——. *Monthly Statistical Bulletin* (various years). Dar es Salaam, Government Printer.

WINTER, H. E.; BEIDELMAN, T. O. 'Tanganyika: A Study of an African Society at National and Local Levels.' In: Julian H. Steward (ed.), *Contemporary Change in Traditional Societies*, Vol. I. Urbana, Ill., University of Illinois Press, 1967.